Praise for
KEVIN ALLEN and
THE HIDDEN AGENDA

"*The Hidden Agenda* makes the invaluable link between understanding your audience's motivation and creating success. It also reveals some of the secret tactics that Kevin has used to help change businesses around the world. It all begins with that simple, timeless practice of connecting with people on a much deeper level. Don't miss the remarkable teachings of this unusual book and author."

—Dan Schawbel, personal branding expert,
bestselling author and owner of
Millennial Branding

"Kevin's enjoyable and informative book reminds us all that to communicate well is to connect with people first."

—Rudy Giuliani, former Mayor of the City of New York

"Kevin Allen is the 'Picasso' of the high art of the new business development and he has finally shared his magical techniques with the rest of us. A must-read!"

—Larry Weber, Chairman and CEO of W2 Group,
author of *Everywhere: Comprehensive Digital
Business Strategy for the Social Media Era*

"Kevin has a special ability to uplift and inspire those around him. His generous spirit is on every page."

—Steven Overman, Vice President and
Global Head Marketing Creation, Nokia

"Anyone who is trying to create the most persuasive selling presentation, the most inspiring vision, or discover the customer sweet spot must read (and re-read) Kevin Allen's new book. While filled with concepts and insights, this is no academic treatise, but a valuable playbook from someone who has 'been there, done that' with amazing success many times."

—Joe Plummer, Professor of Marketing,
Columbia Business School

"Kevin Allen knows the art and science of marketing, brand building, and human persuasion. He shares his unique strategy for winning accounts and building businesses in *The Hidden Agenda*. A must-read tale as only he can tell it."

—Jim R. Heekin III, Chairman and
CEO, Grey Group

"Through the seemingly simple craft of storytelling that connects with human emotions, Kevin leads us one step at a time to a winning strategy. The stories in *The Hidden Agenda* will keep the lessons in your mind long after you have put down the book."

—Kamini Banga, consultant & co-author of
*The 86% Solution: How to Succeed in the Biggest
Market Opportunity of the 21st Century*

"Kevin Allen draws upon more than 25 years of experience in the ad business—across categories and countries—to identify a winning formula for not just pitching an account, but for successfully selling ideas and inspiration. This compelling book is not just for someone who wants to succeed at business; it's for anyone who wants to succeed at life."

—Howard Draft, Executive Chairman, Draftfcb

"Kevin Allen has a powerful ability to turn insight into winning results. In *The Hidden Agenda*, he turns his approach into a discipline we can all use to drive results and win more consistently."   —Andy Janowski, COO, Burberry

"Kevin's knowledge, experience, and humanity were an Interpublic treasure. He is a brilliantly gifted growth practitioner and a natural teacher. It is in his DNA to share. This proves it and *The Hidden Agenda* is a must-read for anyone with growth on their agenda."

—David Bell, Chairman Emeritus,
The Interpublic Group, Advertising Hall
of Fame Inductee (2007)

"*The Hidden Agenda* is an insight into the human agenda of the pitch room and how to turn it to your advantage."

—Jo Tatchell, author of *Diamond in the
Desert* and *The Poet of Baghdad*

"Kevin Allen is a one-of-a-kind person and unequivocally successful in his approach to business growth. Although I would far prefer to have Kevin around the office at all times, *The Hidden Agenda* is a perfect substitute and a great way to have access to his style, generosity, and wisdom."

—Björn Larsson, CMO, SVP, Swedbank

"Kevin Allen's approach unlocks potential within individuals and organizations to realize growth and win business that perhaps in the past has either been a distant thought or considered unobtainable."

—Gary Yates, Operational Excellence,
Civil Aerospace, Rolls-Royce

"Kevin not only speaks and writes eloquently and convincingly, he also puts himself at stake personally and emotionally about things that he believes in. With this book he shares a valuable gift with all of us: his insights and thoughtful advice. Read it."

—Tapio Hedman, Communications Director,
Aalto University Finland

"In *The Hidden Agenda*, Kevin shares his hard won wisdom and shows the power of connecting with your audience. He both inspires and provides the tools to do better today."

—Michael I. Roth, Chairman and CEO,
The Interpublic Group

"Nothing can be sold until you crack your prospect's 'hidden agenda.' Few know how to pitch and uncover what's really going on more than Kevin Allen, adman and pitchman extraordinaire. Whatever you do in business, you've got to learn the art of the pitch. That's why you need to read this book."

—Catherine Kaputa, brand strategist, speaker
and author of *You Are a Brand!* and
Breakthrough Branding

THE
HIDDEN
AGENDA

THE
HIDDEN
AGENDA

A PROVEN WAY TO
WIN BUSINESS AND
CREATE A FOLLOWING

KEVIN ALLEN

bibliomotion
books + media

First published by Bibliomotion, Inc.

711 Third Avenue, New York, NY 10017, USA

2 Park Square, Milton Park, Abingdon, Oxon OX14 4RN, UK

Bibliomotion is an imprint of the Taylor & Francis Group, an informa business

ISBN-13: 978-1-937134-04-4 (hbk)

Library of Congress Control Number: 2012932287

"I Am Not I"

To my brother David Brian Allen, who left us far too soon,
and taught me to see the good in everyone.

Contents

Contents

Foreword

I recently participated in an annual gathering of Chief Marketing Officers in New York City. The presenters, as well as all in attendance, represented a Who's Who of the most valuable brands in the world. The collection of skills, personalities, awards, wealth, responsibilities, influence, and marketing budgets was staggering. If you extended the participants' relationships just two degrees of separation it would likely encompass the majority of today's marketing and media industry.

Being true to form, all the presenters were engaging, intelligent, articulate, and provocative. I was swept up in the highly charged energy of the event and my mind was racing with one new idea after another. Yet, as I reflected on that day somewhat later, an additional insight took form: The agenda was truly representative of what occupies the daily thoughts of CMO's, their marketing organizations, and agency partners: 2D Mobile Barcodes, QR Codes, Social Media Metrics, Run-time Multivariate Decision Platforms, Mobile Marketing Mix, MROI Models, CRM, and a stream of similar technological advances that are collectively reshaping the role of marketing.

Foreword

We have truly entered the marketing 2.0 era and it is a fascinating and energizing time to be immersed in the marketing and advertising professions. But it comes with a cost and, contrary to all the seemingly game changing technological innovations and capabilities at a marketer's disposal, there is an unintended consequence: that the increasing demands of empowered consumers are making it more difficult for CMO's to "control" their brands.

This consequence was palpable and shaped the overall tone of the conference. To add to this stress, CEO's and CFO's have higher expectations for their marketing organizations with these advanced technologies at the heart of the marketing renaissance. What once was a characteristic of truly exceptional marketing leaders—the ability to balance logic with intuition, to use both the right and left brain—appears to be on the wane in light of technology expectations.

Now don't get me wrong. The application of technology in marketing is not a bad thing. It will enable marketing organizations and leaders to secure the seats they should rightfully occupy at the strategic table. My personal credo has always been "the truth is in the numbers" which, when put into practice, is what separates the highly strategic and sought after "Capital M" marketers from tactically capable MARCOM managers. But, the numbers and facts are only a means to an end. Those responsible for building brands are ultimately accountable for creating sustainable consumer or customer value. Making the transition from strategic facts, data, and insights to a unique, differentiating, and emotionally relevant brand promise is the single most difficult step that every marketer and advertising pro must take. The degree of difficulty in doing so is extreme; there is no technology available that will churn out creative solutions with the push of a button and, ultimately, successful transitions from facts to ideas are largely due to the confluence of the right people being in the right place at the right time.

I believe this is the sweet spot that Kevin Allen hits upon in *The Hidden Agenda*. I worked with Kevin and the McCann Erickson team, a collaboration which resulted in the creation of the now iconic MasterCard "Priceless" advertising campaign. We were in the right place at the right time. Along the way, I came to understand that all decisions are both rationally and emotionally based; the emotional benefits usually tips the scale.

Kevin states in *The Hidden Agenda* that everyone is a "pitchman" and that shoe leather is the tried-and-true method to connect ideas and innovation with winning. I couldn't agree more. You will read in the following pages how Kevin applied this philosophy as a McCann Erickson pitchman on one side of the table while myself and the MasterCard team sat on the other side of the table. This is the traditional client-agency scenario one thinks of when talking of new business development. Yet even we "client-types" often play the role of pitch person and employ a bit of shoe leather to secure the win. Every hidden agenda has a back-story, including MasterCard's.

The observation made of MasterCard in *The Hidden Agenda* was that we were maniacally driven to score a big win over our primary credit card competitor, which was very true. The MasterCard brand was in decline in the 1990's and the banks issuing our credit and debit products were losing confidence in the brand's draw with consumers. This was the burning issue when I and my then boss, Nick Utton, proposed a comprehensive agency search process to our banking board members where the consumer's voice would carry the day. The truth would be found in the research numbers. Except for the inconvenient result that everyone's sentimental pick and odds-on favorite—"Priceless"—didn't win the numbers game. The consumer test results did not bear out "Priceless" as the winner. The truth might be in the numbers, but perhaps not the whole truth!

So, I applied the *shoe leather* approach that Kevin talks about here, and visited each of our board directors. I presented the reel of test commercials, reminded them that quantitative consumer test results would determine the winning idea, showed them the final research results…but also recommended the runner-up "Priceless" over the clear and undisputed test winner. One director flat out disagreed with the recommendation and predicted a short, unremarkable life for "Priceless." Yet another suggested that if "Priceless" failed to revive the MasterCard brand then surely the next marketing victim would have the chance to figure it out. By the completion of my road trip, however, the majority agreed with our collective view that "Priceless" was an idea with staying power. It was, and went on to become, much more than a touching TV commercial.

In this scenario, the hidden agenda of the board wasn't very difficult to discern. They wanted the MasterCard brand to be strong so that in turn their consumers would acquire and use the MasterCard products offered by the banks. I sincerely believe, however, beyond this logical business performance rationale there laid an intangible, emotional agenda: the desire to be both an advisor to and participant in a significant inflection point in MasterCard's history. This was much, much more than a routine creative pitch. The directors knew it, Master-Card management knew it, and as demonstrated in *The Hidden Agenda*, Kevin Allen and McCann Erickson knew it. Yes, we honestly believed that MasterCard could win with McCann, as Kevin lays out in his dramatic depiction of the events. And we did. As it turns out, McCann Erickson also won. The agency has become well known and deservingly awarded as the moniker of the creator of "Priceless." McCann readily admits the campaign has opened a few new business doors over the past decade, nothing hidden in that agenda.

The Hidden Agenda reminds me of why I originally headed straight to Madison Avenue—literally—after graduating from college thirty years ago. Kevin's engaging storytelling, deconstruction, and analysis of many highly publicized new business shootouts is riveting to the reader. In addition, he provides thought provoking methods designed to help you read the tea leaves better than all those competing for the same new business win, which is relevant to recent grads and veterans alike.

I now find myself on the forward edge of an emerging trend in higher education by pursuing a second-life as the executive dean for the University of New Haven College of Business. For close to 100 years the school has been graduating many students who have gone on to become notable and successful business leaders. I'm hopeful that my fellow alumni are proud to call me one of theirs. The technologies I mentioned earlier are as familiar to our students today as the new medium of cable television was to me when I studied Marketing & Advertising in college. Possessing strong quantitative skills, the ability to make real-time data based decisions, and knowing your way around a P&L, among other things, are mandatory skills that our future business leaders must possess. But the human side—the lessons included in *The Hidden Agenda*—are equally important and perhaps even more difficult to teach in the conventional sense. I like to tell our students that they will eventually reach a point in their careers where everyone they interact with on the job is smart. A high IQ is compulsory and simply table stakes. The skill that will set them apart is, in fact, their EQ: the emotional quotient that enables them to read a situation, person, or opportunity better than the next person. What they will eventually discover is that *shoe leather* is simply something life and experience teaches you if you pay attention. Having Kevin Allen show the way is simply...

Lawrence Flanagan
New Haven, Connecticut
January 2012

Acknowledgments

This is the last thing I ever thought I would write. That is, I confess I never thought I would see a book in print and it is the thrill of a lifetime. As I put this together, I discovered that this became much more than a chronology of pitch-making, wins and losses, but a stage for the many wonderful people who helped me to believe in myself and taught me so much of what I now have the pleasure to share. It's my joy to bring them to you.

No pitch person ever wins a business alone. It is a total movement of the entire enterprise he/she represents. As catalyst, alchemist, coach, den mother and at times, taskmaster, I relished each pursuit and the thrill of the "yes" decision, of the fine companies who saw that we understood the cherished desire they held close.

In the course of the narrative, I have had the pleasure of including many of the extraordinary people who played a part but there are still others whose contribution both to my career and this book deserve particular recognition.

The first is my mother, Joan Allen. This ray of pure

Acknowledgments

sunshine, of unending support and optimism is a daily tonic. I can't recall just how many evenings were spent reading passages over the phone from London to her unyielding positivity; all echoed by beloved sister Joan and brother Bill, along with "my babies" Jennifer, Diana David, Sarah, John and Ryan.

At McCann, while so many are recalled in the book, I mustn't forget Mark Stewart, every inch a part of the magic that we created and a young star named Peter McGuinness (now a big shot) who somehow seemed to magically make it all happen.

During years at IPG, David Bell, Chairman Emeritus stands out as an unflinching champion as was Larry Weber, a person of immense talent and vision. During my time there, I looked up to the urbane Michael Sennott, but perhaps most of all to the brilliant Bruce Nelson, who never failed to challenge and inspire and I might add, albeit sheepishly, taught me how to dress properly.

I thank my dear friend Steve Rabin for planting the seed of forming my company, to wonderful Rose Fass for inspiration and clarity, to Catherine Kaputa, coach and author who helped my get the book off the ground and colleagues like Jay Mandelbaum of JP Morgan Chase who always told me I could do it.

The enormous task of writing was made a joy with people like author Jo Tachell, my dear colleagues Nikki Fiveash, Hugues Quesnel and Claudie Plen of KevinAllenPartners and especially my good friend John Cutler, who was one part encourager and three parts tough guy, but highly supportive critic. He made such a difference even though at time I confess I didn't want to hear it.

I simply cannot thank Larry Flanagan, former celebrated CMO of MasterCard (and now a Dean!) for his enthusiastic support and for his wonderful foreword.

All the while, from my adopted "family" in London, the

excellent input from psychotherapist Hopeton Shaw on Jung and human desire and the effervescent encouragement from Victoria Wilson James with the constant cry of "You go, Big Daddy Guru!"

Most of all, I would not have written a word, or accomplished a fraction of any of it were it not for my partner Karl. I wrote this in the first instance because of him, his daily challenge, encouragement and steady counsel, along with just simple brilliant thinking. I owe more to him than words could ever say.

To all of you, I say thank you, from the bottom of my heart.

INTRODUCTION

The Heart of the Matter

For more than four months we fought. More than twenty advertising agencies were shown off the field. We battled against another five, including the odds-on favorite, for a final place in the pitch lineup for this prestigious account. Unexpectedly, we found ourselves in a dead heat with a downtown rival. This had become one of the most-watched competitions in the U.S. advertising business. The prize: over $100 million in fees and a place of glory among our peers. We wrestled day after day, up and down blind alleys, toiling to find a winning idea. Just like our downtown nemesis, we knew that lives would change, and change big, for whoever won this business. The day of presentations came and went. So much preparation and anticipation was over in a flash. Then came the wait.

The call came. But it only added further agony by announcing that our recommended idea would, in the jargon of the advertising business, "go into research." This meant that for several more weeks we would wait, while the fruits of our labor were pitted in consumer focus groups against those of our rival. May the best idea win! Well, word reached us and the news was not good. We were being outscored by our rivals. The terms laid down in the final stages of the competition were clear. The other agency would be declared the winner.

The phone rang. "We need to talk. We've got problems. It's only right we talk in person." Our hearts sank. We braced ourselves for the inevitable. Perhaps it wasn't so surprising. I began to think, What should we have done differently? What was missing? What did we overlook? On the day of the meeting, four clients, somber-faced, ushered us into the boardroom. They took their places across from us in the enormous conference room.

We faced them, literally squirming in our seats. "This has been very difficult," an executive began. "We know how hard it has been but sometimes things just don't work out the way you think. We're sorry to say..." At that moment the Master-Card executives reached into their briefcases and in unison drew out four bottles of champagne bearing the phrase *"A Priceless Moment"* emblazoned on their labels. "We're sorry to say you're stuck with us now."

How did we win this business? Why didn't MasterCard hand the business to the agency with the winning score? Was it because we knew more about credit cards? Or was it because we had a slicker presentation? It was neither. We won the MasterCard account because everything about the now famous "Priceless" campaign pitch was rooted in what I call the *hidden agenda* of the MasterCard team: *a desire to, for once, triumph over the seemingly unstoppable Visa.* This unspoken, visceral, emotional core was a central motivator behind the company's search for an advertising partner. Larry Flanagan, a key decision maker who went on to become MasterCard's celebrated marketing director, observed, "We knew there was a big idea in 'Priceless,' but what counted as much was we felt they were a team that could win."

2

Life as a Pitchman

My mom has never really been able to understand exactly what I do. She is immensely proud, but I'm unable to provide her with a simple and "braggable" occupation title, like, "My son, the doctor, or my son, the lawyer." Finally, with the phenomenon of MasterCard's "Priceless" marketing campaign fully ensconced in popular culture, she has a sense of what I do. While I reiterated time and again that I was the pitch guy in the mix, she became convinced I dreamt up the whole campaign. I tried for some time to dissuade her, trying to describe the role of the pitch guy in the process. I gave up. So, with sincere apologies to the geniuses who gave rise to "Priceless," I no longer attempt to dissuade her.

I grew up in the tough hallways of the toughest ad agency in the competitive field of advertising, McCann Erickson. Miscast as a sensitive and soft-spoken guy in a sharp-elbowed environment, I became the company's successful new business winner. It was not because I learned to be like the others, but because I learned to apply natural gifts of human empathy and an ability to sense what was in the hearts of my buyers. I somehow knew instinctively that if I connected the company and our strengths to the client's emotional needs, we would be chosen. This was not an act of persuasion, but rather a process of creating a profound human bond. By doing this, we won; and we did win, much of the time.

Yes, I was and am a pitch guy. In fact, if you press Mom to describe what I do, she asserts, "That kid could sell refrigerators in the Antarctic!" I now know, after all these years, that she is right, and it's not through any techniques or tricks but because of certain gifts I have been given. I have a sort of emotional x-ray vision. It's an ability to instinctively read people. Over the course of twenty-five years, this innate sense became the means by which I could understand and connect with the emotional motivations of my advertising buyers. It might seem crazy to hear from the likes of me, but I can confidently conclude after scores upon scores of pitches, that people are not *persuaded* to buy your idea, your company, or your product. They are, however, compelled to follow you because you have made a profound connection with what lies in their hearts.

After I won an account, I had the privilege of going to dinner with our new client, and after a while (often after a few glasses of wine), I would ask the same question: *Why did you pick us?* The answer was always the same: *"Because you get it."* Get it? Get what? The "what" is the *hidden agenda*, the emotional motivator behind all the statistics, the business jargon, and the other things that surround any key business issue. It is how people in fact make decisions, with their hearts. Whereas I first thought it a business weakness that I was sensitive and intuitive, it actually became a potent business asset, one that will only increase in importance as time progresses.

Over the years I learned to apply this special gift and to codify my approach into *The Hidden Agenda* method for my colleagues to build on. When I began my company, which is set up to help people grow themselves and their companies using these techniques, an exuberant friend of mine, Chris Weil, exclaimed, "You gotta write this down! You're the billion dollar man!" Now, I think Chris in his characteristic enthusiasm may have gotten a decimal point slightly in the wrong place, but I can say with all humility that I have used the hidden agenda approach to lead literally dozens of pitches that have won hundreds of millions of dollars in revenues for the ad agencies where I worked. I relentlessly chased growth in my years with the mad men (and women) of McCann Erickson, with advertising holding company The Interpublic Group, and ad agency Lowe Worldwide, winning accounts like Smith Barney, Nestlé, L'Oréal, Lufthansa, Johnson & Johnson, JP Morgan Chase, Marriott, Opel, South African Airways, Pfizer, Deutsche Bank, Microsoft, Credit Suisse, and others. Later, in my years with the advertising holding company The Interpublic Group, I pitched dozens of companies, including the likes of Nokia and Computer Associates. Global ad agency Lowe Worldwide, where I was vice-chairman, made *Ad Age*'s "Turnaround Agency of the Year" in 2009, in no small measure because we pitched and won clients such as Unilever, Nestlé, Sharp, Ericsson, Becks, Electrolux, AEG, Zanussi, and China Mobile.

The principles of my approach were formed and tested during my beginnings in the kitchens of Marriott International and in my formative days of pitching to Bernie's Frozen Hors d'oeuvres in Hoboken, New Jersey. They served me in my years chasing growth with McCann Erickson and with the dozens of companies around the world I pitched to in my years with the Interpublic Group. I saw these principles at work as an advisor in Rudy Giuliani's "New York Miracle" and during the highs of our famous campaign of MasterCard's "Priceless" ads; I saw them at work in pitches to venerable brands like Johnson & Johnson and to emerging global companies like China Mobile.

These techniques also made their special mark in people's lives, including mine. You'll see how a group from Soweto shared their ambitions for a new nation in a pitch for South African Airways, and how we shared in the fight for AIDS testing that transformed social policy, or how a pitch for a faltering credit card changed lives, or how a team of people came together with the mission to relieve chronic pain. Life-changing and game-changing experiences, all. After these and countless others in my twenty-five years on the frontlines of pitching for my supper, I decided it was time to share my experiences. Instead of running around the globe in pursuit of new business, I founded a company that coaches, trains, and prepares businesses of all shapes and sizes to pitch effectively. The pitching skills I have learned that have served me so well are all in this book. I dedicate them to you.

What Is This Book About?

From babies to banks, from Singapore to Saudi Arabia, I've worked for twenty-five years with clients to create growth that spanned cultural divides, various business sectors, and diverse circumstances. Pitching took me to the foot of the Capitol building in Washington, D.C., and to worldwide gatherings where I evangelized along with the greatest of business gurus. I have counseled, coached, and spoken all over the world about pitching and, perhaps most rewarding of all, I have had the privilege of coaching young, ambitious minds, calling upon them to join the ranks of successful pitch people everywhere.

In all these years, the single most important thing I learned is that there is no magic formula, trick, or technique of hypnotic persuasion that will make people do anything you say like a bunch of zombies. Instead, behind every decision to buy—whether the item is a service or a product, an argument or an idea—is an unspoken emotional motivation. This is the *hidden agenda*. People don't follow you because they've been hoodwinked; they follow you because they believe in you.

They employ you, promote you, buy from you, or hire you because you understand their values, their wants, and their needs. It doesn't matter how or where the pitch is delivered, or what it is you have to sell. People will make an active decision to follow you based upon the way you resonate with their hidden agendas. Understanding and connecting to the powerful emotions that underlie the hidden agenda is the first and most important step you can take toward winning the business and the following you intend. This book is about how to unlock your target's hidden agenda and connect your core strengths, values, and ambitions with your prospect in a way that resonates, engages, and wins.

Who Should Read This Book?

In a word: everyone. Each of us pitches every day. A successful pitch can mean quietly motivating a hesitant client, one on one, or it can mean mobilizing an entire organization, heart and soul, to put every ounce of its abilities on display. Sometimes we pitch to a small room full of skeptical colleagues. Other times we pitch to a boss, or to a board of directors, or to a new organization. Sometimes we pitch an idea or a vision. Other times we pitch a service, or a hundred million dollars–worth of high-tech equipment. Every pitch involves the fundamental belief that behind every sale is an unspoken emotional motivation.

This book is for leaders of all types. The head of any organization is its ultimate pitch person, pitching for loyalty and for uniting around a common direction, a belief system, a *real ambition*. Conventional wisdom among the ranks of business gurus suggest that if the majority of employees can articulate the values and direction of the organization, then the company will outperform its peers exponentially. I'd say it another way: If you can see into the hearts of your people and understand and connect with their hidden agendas, their emotional motivation, you can mobilize them to accomplish anything.

This refinement of pitch isn't a once-in-a-while thing. It ranges from the informal meetings we have with colleagues and clients each and every day to the momentous acts associated with leading huge organizations to accomplish the seemingly impossible. As a leader, your principle job is to stir people to join you and to act.

This book is written by an adman, but it is for any of you out there with a story to tell and a pitch to make. You might be a young graduate on the frontlines, moving up your company's ladder and contributing toward its prosperity, or you might be a CEO steering a turnaround. You might be part of a community of new entrepreneurs created by the economic earthquakes of the last several years. Perhaps you are leading a foundation or a not-for-profit, or are rallying a community to drive a vital issue. Maybe you are running for office. No matter which leadership profile fits you, you will be leading your organization into new unknowns and uncharted waters.

I call all you dreamers, strivers, fighters, doers, and itchy-feet people "growth aspirants." You are optimists who can see possibilities. You're quest people, on a journey toward a goal of personal and professional enrichment, who believe that the place they seek can be reached. I am willing to bet you share a common ambition: to sell your ideas, to grow the enterprises you are a part of, and to grow yourselves with it. *Your ability to pitch is the very spearpoint and lifeblood of achieving these ambitions.*

This book is for you.

Why Now?

We now enter an era of what I call *pure growth*. Pure growth is not deals, mergers, cost-cutting, or balance sheet gymnastics. It is the basics, the fundamentals of any business, big or small. It focuses on the customer; the crystallization of a great idea; the development of an innovation that represents true value; and the channeling of company efforts, from the executive suite to the loading dock, to sell that innovation with passion. Pure growth is not a financial game, it is a people game. It is an inspired subject. It flows from a wellspring of ambition pursued with passion.

The economic downturn of the last few years is a long-awaited reckoning. Growth, as it was heralded, was brought to us by mergers, deal making, acquisition, hedging, betting, and balance sheet tricks. *There's only one way out: shoe leather.* "Shoe leather," by which I mean real live selling to the real live needs of a buyer, is the foundation of solid growth. "Shoe leather growth," then, is about the simple, vital elements at the core of commerce. It is about creation, passion, and pursuit. It is propelled by good-hearted persuasiveness and the discipline to deliver honorably. And this philosophy is not restricted to those whose job description is to sell. It requires the mobilization of everyone in the organization. The question is, How do you reach them?

Every buyer buys with his heart, not with his head, and in every heart lies a hidden agenda. No doubt, we must be masters of the contemporary means by which we engage with our communities and with our customers. That's staying current and relevant. No matter how complex the selling landscape is, at the root of the sale are human beings with *desires.*

This unspoken, visceral, emotional core is the true motivator behind every pitch. When you unlock it and connect your strengths, beliefs, and ambitions that resonate with the hidden agenda, you win.

The Amazing Enid

In my childhood, I remember the dozens of "shoe leather" people who showed up at our door on a regular basis selling everything from milk to vacuum cleaners. Some were familiar, like the Fuller Brush man, who would whiz by, calling out to my mother, "Need anything today, Mrs. Allen?" Each and every one of these individuals who was working in a time-honored and, I think, noble profession were good, hard-working people out there pitching to make a living while trying to make our lives just a little bit easier.

"I'm putting myself through college…selling the book of knowledge." This little ditty is one folks would sing in amusement about the salesmen (and women) who arrived at the doorstep with Brylcreem in their hair and an encyclopedia under their arm. While researching this book, I decided to try to find a real-life, honest-to-goodness, door-to-door salesperson from this era, the fifties. Through my mother's over-sixty-five dance troupe (you can't make this stuff up), I hit pay dirt, a marvelous woman in the form of one Enid Merin, of Levittown, New York (I presumed her to be in her late seventies, but one never asks such questions). Enid had sold a number of products door to door throughout her career, notably *The World Book Encyclopedia*.

Listening to this remarkable woman speak about pitching was like listening to Einstein talk about relativity. The essential elements of understanding and connecting to a hidden agenda were woven throughout the compelling basics laid out by this energetic and charming lady.

First, Enid decided *who* her target was.

"As I approach the door of the house, I started by noticing small details so I could qualify them, for example if there was a fresh net in the basketball hoop this would indicate the presence of children in the home."

Enid understood that, no matter how complex the selling landscape, at the root of a successful pitch are human beings with *wants, needs, and values.* Her aim was to understand the emotional makeup of her potential customers.

"It's very simple, Kevin, it's about desires," Enid commented. *"A young mother may want a set of encyclopedias, but she desires for her kid to become president."*

Once she understood *who* she was dealing with, Enid set about finding *what* would connect emotionally with her audience. Her aim was to forge a bond with the individuals to whom she was pitching. For Enid, aspiring mothers who wished the world for their children would, by definition, be a group who valued the advantages that encyclopedias would bring. Ultimately, these women would respond to somebody who, like Enid, had a profound belief in the intrinsic value of the product she was selling.

"I loved what I was selling. It wasn't schlock. I truly believe the best gift you can give your kids is the advantage of a good education. A young mind without the opportunity for knowledge

and education is a terrible waste and I knew that I could make a difference."

Of course, Enid's pitch process ultimately could not have been successful without superb communication skills. *How* Enid delivered her pitch was a key part of her success. She built an argument, demonstrated passion for what she believed in, and communicated in the right tone with language that resonated with her targets.

"Good morning. My name is Enid Merin and I represent World Book Encyclopedia. *I imagine you have an entertainment center in your home, but do you have an education center? May I step in?"*

Enid affirmed my unwavering belief that the pitch, to be effective, is rooted in fundamental human truths that lie in the very hearts of your audience. Underpinning the success of the amazing Enid and every other successful shoe leather person is a simple but far-reaching logic:

A pitch is always about your target's wants or needs, or about the values they hold close.
Wants, needs, and values are locked into your target's hidden agenda.
Unlocking your target's hidden agenda wins the pitch.

In other words, if you shape your pitch based on the emotional motivation that lies in the hidden agenda of your target, you'll win. Of course, this isn't to say that the quality of what you are selling is unimportant. Delivering whatever great product or service you have promised is a given. But let's move beyond the belief that your pitch is exclusively about the product or the service. What you have to pitch only has value if it resonates with your target's hidden agenda. I have seen many a pitch for a technically brilliant idea go down in flames because it had nothing whatsoever to do with the target's *real* reason for being interested in the product or service. Building a better mousetrap is essential, but only when you pitch it effectively can you guarantee you'll win every time. Like Enid, the best pitch people understand their target's *emotional motivation*, have an abiding *belief* in what they are selling, and put on a show...*they tell a story*. This book looks in detail at each element in a winning formula: the *who*, the *what*, and the *how* that comprise every effective shoe leather pitch.

How Is This Book Organized?

The Hidden Agenda is designed to be easy to follow and implement. Part 1 of this book looks at the *who*. These chapters are about your audience and the hidden agenda that drives them. These individuals have needs, wants, and values. They may be collected together in a community of like-minded people who share common beliefs and value systems. Pitching effectively to them requires digging deep to understand the emotional, visceral, and unstated emotional motivation that lies in their hearts. Chapter 1 explores what the hidden agenda is and how to conceptualize it in a *hidden agenda statement*. Chapter 2 looks at how to conceptualize the hidden agendas of large communities of buyers into a *conceptual target*. Chapter 3 is packed with practical techniques and strategies for uncovering and elucidating your target's hidden agenda.

Part 2 is about the *what*. This is about finding the *leverageable assets* that connect emotionally with your audience. When you connect your *leverageable assets* to the *hidden agenda* of your buyer, you win. This alchemy is a result of a careful and disciplined distillation of who you are and what makes you special. An essential element in developing your pitch is to reach in and find the special character and uniqueness that makes you who you are. It is not being something that you are not. It is finding and bringing forward, in compelling terms, what makes you special and connecting to an audience who values it. Chapter 4 looks at your *core*. These are your true and compelling assets, the rich mosaic of characteristics you possess that your target will be drawn to and will bond with through affinity and even a little bit of curiosity. Your *core* is your unique ability and the strengths that separate you from others. Chapter 5 explores your *credo*, your beliefs and value systems. Successful pitches express the abiding and sincere beliefs of the individual or company making that pitch. Shared beliefs win pitches. Chapter 6 addresses your *real ambition*. Your real ambition is your desire to create something good where nothing existed before. It is a measure of your worth, and of the worth of your organization. You will be chosen because your special ambitions ignite those of your buyer.

Part 3 of the book looks at the *how*. This is assembling your pitch with crystal clear logic and delivering it in an engaging and memorable way. A pitch is not a mere communications undertaking. It is a means to mobilize an individual or a community of people to follow you and to embrace where you are going. A powerful pitch inspires your target to engage with the product or services you offer, and to essentially vote for you now and in the future. Chapter 7 looks at your *win strategy* and explores how your *core, credo,* and *real ambition* can be strategically communicated in clear, compelling, and engaging terms. Chapter 8 identifies the *advocate's approach* to building an unbeatable argument. Chapter 9 explores how to demonstrate passion and strike the right tone that resonates and moves your audience to join you through the *power of storytelling*.

 ## How to Use This Book

I have been very lucky to have had wonderful mentors. Some kindhearted, others grumpy (but still kindhearted); all had rich experience, a great deal of talent, and most of all a generous desire to share. They are a very tough act to follow, and though I'll never be quite like them, I somehow feel that now it's my turn. So think of this book not as a star-studded tale of my exploits or a list of to-dos, but as coaching in print. I will lay out for you the alchemy of moving an audience, no matter who they are. Oh, and to help the cause further, when you see this icon (see KAPTV above) you can go to *www.kevinallenpartners.com/video* and view supporting videos from yours truly expanding on some the key concepts throughout the book.

These days I do a lot of coaching. I think it is helpful not only to lay out how things evolved for me—the key ideas and step-by-step techniques that worked—but also to offer assurance that if a gangling and under-confident kid from nowhere like me can acquire the knack, I guarantee you can, too. A successful pitch is not glibness or slick show biz, but a studied empathy with what truly lies in the heart of your target, as well as the courage to be yourself and to match what makes you special with this hidden agenda. When you make this kind of connection, they'll choose you. My hope is that you use this book for its broad principles, as steady guidance, and as a handy pitch-to-pitch field manual, but maybe most importantly, I hope that it serves as a constant reminder *that you can pitch and do it brilliantly.*

And Now...

This whole book is about something I call the *hidden agenda*, so let's start with a definition of what it is, and what comprises it.

REMEMBER THIS

Every single day we sell ourselves, our ideas, or the companies and products we represent. These pitches range from the informal meetings we have with colleagues and clients each and every day to the momentous tasks associated with leading huge organizations to accomplish the seemingly impossible. These all require that you stir people to join you, and to act. Connect to the *hidden agenda*, the profound, unspoken desire that lies in the heart of your constituency, and you can move mountains.

PART I

WHO? FINDING THE HIDDEN AGENDA

1

Defining the Hidden Agenda

. . . .

The *hidden agenda* is the unspoken, emotional motivation that resides in the heart of your audience. This
emotional core is the true motivator behind every
decision.

*"The 'want' is the rational part, but 'desire,' that's the emotional
part. It's the emotional part that buys,"* pitch lady Enid Merin
says. The pitch is an entirely human endeavor. It is about
people, about their ambitions, fears, and desires. The people
who best understand these underlying motivators will win.
The successes my companies had in business development
during my time at ad agencies were due to fabulous teams and
great products, but also in no small measure to our scientific
approach to what I call the *hidden agenda.*

Carpe Diem

When the MasterCard people walked into our conference room on the day of our pitch, we displayed two huge words on the screen, *"Carpe Diem."* Nat Puccio, a brilliant strategic mind, (and Sicilian born, as he is quick to add) took the floor. This formidable, highly intense native Brooklynite spoke: "You see these words before you? They mean 'seize the day.' It is because this is your day…your time. You will stigmatize Visa's platform of conspicuous consumption and become the preferred card in customers' wallets, but most importantly in their hearts."

Then a slide clicked into place, and this slide read: *"Coke versus Pepsi, AT&T versus MCI."* Nat went on, "You see these logos before you? They represent the successful battles we waged against Pepsi on behalf of our Coca-Cola client, and the telecom war we waged against MCI. There's nothing we love more than a good fight, and we are not accustomed to losing."

You could hear a pin drop.

Why was this opening scripted in such, bold, confident, even combative terms? The fiercely competitive stance was based on the hidden agenda that we had established for Master-Card. Their visceral desire was, after fifteen years of loss after loss to Visa, to finally become winners. Nothing less than a complete victory would do. Victory would come at the expense of Visa. We spoke passionately about our recommendation, but more importantly we spoke about our ability to help them succeed. Our pitch resonated around the room as Nat spoke because it resonated in their hearts. When I asked Larry Flanagan, who went on to become MasterCard's celebrated CMO, about their decision to award us the business, he said, "We bonded because McCann understood the deep desire of the MasterCard customer, but they understood ours, too. We knew we could win with those guys." The "Priceless" campaign that was presented in this meeting has become arguably one of the best known and most applauded brand campaigns in recent decades.

MasterCard's Hidden Agenda

The opportunity to pitch for MasterCard began nearly a year before our pitch meeting, thanks to the relentless efforts of one of the industry's best new business people, Margie Altschuler, my alter ego and partner in crime. She chased the MasterCard people relentlessly for months (you *don't* say no to Margie). After an extensive screening review of dozens of agencies, MasterCard selected six to pitch in the final presentation. All of the competing ad agencies were invited to a briefing, a meeting at which the client shares its business situation and the "assignment" for competitors to work toward. As you can imagine, this is a process that makes slightly skittish ad people very uncomfortable indeed. Imagine archrivals all in the same room, receiving the same briefing and having to be on their best behavior while, when the client was not looking, they glared at one another. I was elected chief snarler.

The MasterCard delegation was headed by Nick Utton, a confident and engaging fellow who declared the essential problem for MasterCard was its "emotional bankruptcy." For our team, this was a clear and unmistakable insight, one that we later could see was the key to solving their seemingly impossible marketing problem. My kindred spirit was Larry Flanagan, who was generous of spirit and encouraging but also kept us focused. I bonded with him instantly.

After the briefing was over we were invited to a luncheon at which agency executives were dispersed among the MasterCard clients at several round tables in the hotel ballroom. The task, we were told, would be to enjoy lunch and to take the opportunity to ask questions of MasterCard executives. At regular twenty-minute intervals, one of the clients clinked a glass (like at a wedding, only none of the agencies kissed...), at which time the agencies' executives rotated to the next table so they could meet and ask questions of other individuals on the MasterCard team. Business development speed dating!

In the course of my dates, er, meetings, I met several key people from MasterCard. I asked one about his views of Visa and its marketing prowess. Instinctively, I was looking to see how he felt in his heart about his chief rival and to learn his feelings about MasterCard's prospects for competing effectively against Visa. My reason for asking this in particular was a consequence of a fact shared in the briefing: for fifteen years, MasterCard had been unable to score any meaningful gain or victory against its archrival. The response: "They're tough, real tough. It's going to take some doing to make the gains we need to make." The other gentleman I spoke with had a slightly different take: "If we can pull off reversing the Visa juggernaut, we'll make history." And still another: "If we don't get this right, we won't be here in eighteen months." It struck me then and there that the hidden agenda of these delightful folks from MasterCard was one part ambition, one part worry. My encapsulation of this thinking was the following hidden agenda:

"We need to score a victory over Visa in the marketplace and in doing so be famous for it...but the odds are stacked against us."

This simple insight from the depths of their hearts provided the backdrop for a presentation that would be based on raw ambition, a good bit of daring, and supreme confidence as seasoned and grizzled competitors. The manner in which we pursued our solution from a marketing perspective, our view of how we would seize opportunities in the marketplace for them, as well as the design, tone, and shape of the very presentation we made on that fateful day, were driven by the hidden agenda that burned in their hearts. For the MasterCard people to decide in our favor, given all that was at stake, took a huge amount of courage. As I look back on my career, I can think of few others who have demonstrated such bravery. Said Larry Flanagan, MasterCard's CMO, "In the end, we let our instincts rule, to embrace 'Priceless,' an idea that testing said had failed, and also to embrace a group that understood what was in the heart of the MasterCard customer as well as ours."

A Motivation Named Desire

When I was coming up in the business, it seemed to me that daily life and business life were two completely separate animals. The person I was and the way I conducted myself in my private life, including how I approached decision making, changed radically the moment I walked through the doors of mighty McCann. I was led to believe that success in business involved a mastery of cold hard facts and brutal logic. Sheer nonsense. Whether in private life or in business, we are all driven by fundamental human impulses and desires. They rule our hearts and play a primary role in the way we make decisions. This includes decisions about the people we hire, the directions we take, the people we choose to follow, and the organizations we elect to join. It is human desire and emotion that are at the core of every decision. Facts offer support and proof of the rightness of our instincts and the clarity of our desire.

Much smarter minds than mine have delved into the subject of desire and human motivation. From Abraham Maslow and his hierarchy of needs to Carl Jung and his identification of personality types and unconscious drives, to those who hold more contemporary views on the human psyche, all, I think, would agree that deeply held desires are fundamental to the human drive. For me, the root of desire is hope.

"Hope springs eternal." This wonderful phrase was one of the many extraordinary replies I heard my mother give to the never-ending questions we kids would pose about our family's future. When we wanted to know whether my dad would get the job or whether the Mets would win, this was her reply. It is what we came to expect from this amazing woman; she taught us that tomorrow could very well bring good things. Positivity and possibility are fundamental to the human spirit, and when you examine people's deepest desires, they inevitably revolve around hopes for what the future could bring. People follow you because they believe that not only do you understand the hopes they have in their hearts, but *you in fact can help to make them come true.*

The Hidden Agenda Defined

I first became aware of the term *hidden agenda* through a wonderful woman named Helene Kalmanson. Helene was a business development consultant called into the agency I was working with at the time. A formidable but charming lady, she took me to lunch and told me the following: "Kevin, I need to tell you, you have a bright career ahead of you, however prepare yourself that you will be grossly misunderstood. You're a genuinely nice person, but people in this business can't imagine anybody in the business who is, so they will initially think you are full of baloney." She went on to urge me not to change one bit. She showed me that my gifts of human empathy and the ability to sense the hearts of the people I met would become my greatest business assets. Given the "mad men" environment I was in at the time, I actually thought that *she* was full of baloney, but after the passage of time and dozens upon dozens of successful new business pursuits, I realize now how right she was. Thank you, Helene.

The hidden agenda lies at the heart of every pitch. It is the nucleus that joins your pitch with its audience. The person who can exercise greatest sensitivity to the prospect's hidden agenda will be declared the winner. To be effective, a winning pitch must find, tune into, lock onto, and ignite that agenda. No matter how fabulous your team or how great your product, no pitch will ever be successful and no recommendation ever accepted unless the fundamental desires that underpin your buyer's hidden agenda are inextricably woven into the process.

Everyone has a desire, an ambition, a belief, or a worry that drives her decisions. Each of us has deep-rooted longings that yearn to be satisfied. These visceral, often unspoken, desires are fundamental to any decision we make or direction we take. Emotions and desires locked into a hidden agenda are as varied as the people in the world. The hidden agenda may include the desire to be recognized, to feel appreciated, to create something, to be admired, to lead, or to feel safe and secure. These desires are at the root of the way people behave and are the lens through which people make choices. A hidden agenda comes in all shapes and sizes, but it is always present and always vital.

Out of Plain View

The question is, why is this desire or motive hidden from view? In any business setting the social pressures and dynamics follow established organizational norms. The coldly analytic and rational business decision maker, as a persona, cannot be seen as bowing to frail emotion to render decisions about things of business consequence. For a very long time there has been tremendous social convention inside organizations that dictates that one should not be anything other than stoically "professional." Many I speak with say that culture still exists. There is far too much at stake, some might argue, for the "instability" of pure emotion to rule over the rational elements of business decision making. Yet, in fact, it does. It just doesn't show. Fully in touch with their feelings about their circumstances and how those feelings of desire, whether ambition or fear, might be perceived by others, business executives keep them from view. But make no mistake, the feelings are there.

The Needle in the Haystack

The other important point to consider is that many pitch people do not undertake the search for the hidden agenda. Instead, they view the rational problem as the single issue to be tackled. Clearly, every pursuit I ever undertook had as its objective the solution of a client's particular business problem.

The difference, though, is that every problem or opportunity takes place in a *context*. The business problem or opportunity is a human issue linked to the underlying want, need, or value system the client holds close. These vital elements of the hidden agenda are the filters through which their decisions will be made. *To win a business or to create your following is to link these two vital elements together.* When you do, you win.

The power of the search for your audience's hidden agenda lies in your ability not only to identify it, but also to connect to it. In doing so, your audience instantly realizes that you understand them and what they truly seek. But how do you identify the hidden agenda they hold so close?

The Three Hidden Agendas

While there are as many hidden agendas as there are desires, in my experience they can be grouped into one of three categories, *wants*, *needs*, or *values*. Let's look first at wants and needs. These are based upon a person's fundamental level of confidence; that is, they might be "leaning toward"—viewing their circumstances through the lens of ambition and confidence—or "leaning back"—viewing circumstances through the lens of fear or concern.

Wants

The desire found in the hidden agenda of the want category is based on ambition. It reflects confidence and a positive view of what the future might bring. The people you encounter may not be able to articulate what the future looks like (that's where you come in!), but they look forward to it. People with a hidden agenda based on want will respond to bold gestures. They will want to feel that you understand their business and can see what they see, and that you share in the excitement of the goal they seek and the journey toward its attainment

Needs

The hidden agenda of needs is based on a fear and a desire for something that is lacking. It is the desire of longing. There is a feeling in the hidden agenda of need that something is missing, that there is an essential ingredient lacking that is necessary to function. There is a sense of urgency surrounding the hidden agenda of needs, and this agenda includes a call for confidence. Individuals whose hidden agendas are based on needs are reticent and cautious. They need a good deal of assurance, and need to see confidence in you and your ability to deliver something that they lack.

Values

The roots of the hidden agenda for people who are motivated by values are their deeply held beliefs. For them, the issue will always be how they set, calibrate, and measure their actions in accordance with the compass of their value system.

For a long while I thought that the hidden agenda essentially came in two flavors, wants and needs. There were a number of circumstances, however, where prospects viewed the world entirely through the lens of value systems that they held close. Now, while it's true that they no doubt had a want or a need, what really motivated them emotionally was a special belief system that arched over everything. I found this to be true of the folks from Marriott Corporation, a company I was a proud member of early in my career and whose values I admire greatly, as well as those from Johnson & Johnson, a company whose very belief system is etched in stone.

The Baby's Upside Down

Fortune had it that we were invited to pitch for a prestigious financial services account, the venerable Smith Barney. This was a big opportunity for us to develop a campaign in the footsteps of one of the great financial services advertising campaigns summarized in a line, *"They make money the old-fashioned way. They earn it."* This storied idea was made famous by an execution involving the late John Houseman, a gruff-speaking British actor who became known in the film *The Paper Chase*. In the film he played a demanding college professor who exhorted students to work hard and not take shortcuts. In character, he was a perfect spokesman. At the end of each commercial he summarized Smith Barney's point of view that money was made through old-fashioned principles of diligence and hard work. There was a parallel, we thought, that the value systems of Smith Barney's inherent integrity was evident in the group that we met and would present to some weeks later. While clearly among some of Wall Street's biggest figures, what struck me about these individuals was their common cultural glue. These folks were grounded, open, principled, and just plain decent.

As we worked on our strategy, we recognized that the people who made up the Smith Barney customer base were people
who identified with this value system. They were self-made
and entrepreneurial types who knew that money doesn't grow
on trees and yet there was issue over how to deliver the notion
of old-fashioned ideals, while at the same time giving the company a more contemporary, modern appearance. Our idea was
to develop television commercials using a series of avant-garde
photographs which taken together would reflect, in abstract,
the core values of thrift, hard work, and diligence. One of
these, in a sort of Avedon-esque style was a little family: father,
mother, and three kids, the smallest of whom was a baby held
upside down by the dad. It was a striking and, we thought, very
arresting image. On presentation day our strategic team delivered an impassioned exposé about the Smith Barney customer
who believed that everything they had was a consequence of
hard work, discipline, and sweat. After this we then moved to
the presentation of our "photograph" campaign. No sooner
did the little family photograph appear, an immediate question
emerged from our audience:

"Why is the baby upside down?"

"Well, it contemporizes the execution."

"Yes, but the blood is rushing to the baby's head!"

"Ah, well it's avant-garde..."

"Yeah, but it's an upside-down baby!"

We looked at each other, squirming in our seats, but
instinctively fought hard for our belief in the execution that we
developed and argued that, inverted babies notwithstanding,
the contemporary nature of our execution would modernize
Smith Barney.

We stuck to our guns, and left crestfallen that we had gone

down in flames. There would be no way on earth that we could get over the upside-down child affair. When the call came:

"Kevin. Here's the decision. You got the business...lose the baby!"

They unanimously agreed that, execution aside, what impressed them most was our conviction and willingness to fight for our beliefs. The members of the client team were the kind of people who would expect us to stand up for our convictions, a belief they valued themselves. As I reflect back, the business was won not because of the product we took in the room but because we connected with the *hidden agenda* of a shared value system:

"We value standing up for what we think is right."

In the years that followed, I learned that the key to winning, or reaching any audience you wish to motivate and to join you, is not through anything other than to the heart, by genuinely connecting to the wants, needs, or beliefs they hold close. It was a powerful lesson.

The hidden agenda is not reserved just for business pitches. It is universal in its application. One of my most profound career experiences is also one where the elements of the hidden agenda were very much at work.

The Rotten Apple

In 1993, I was at McCann Erickson in New York, a young account director working on the AT&T account. During this time I met a man named Herbert Rickman, a key figure as special assistant to New York City Mayor Ed Koch. We met by chance when a few colleagues of mine and I agreed to create a pro bono advertising campaign to combat teen pregnancy. It proved to be a smash, we all ended up featured in *Newsweek*, Herb and I went on to become great friends, and he became my mentor. One of Herb's frequent tricks was to call me at the last minute to meet him at lunches with the most amazing people. "Schmendrick!" (his name for me, and, for that matter, most people), he would say, "Cancel what you're doing and meet me for lunch at Cipriani, and don't be late!" I would dutifully follow his instructions, attending countless lunches and meeting some of the most extraordinary people imaginable. (At that lunch, incidentally, it was Fay Wray, of *King Kong* and the Empire State Building fame.)

So, true to form, Herb called one Friday morning and said the usual, only this time it was, "Second Avenue Deli, lunch, dress nice, Schmendrick, and follow my lead." In a suit and tie, I arrived and was shown to a table where sat Rudy Giuliani and what were clearly formidable city titans. Herb beamed. "Gentlemen, I want you to meet one of advertising's giants and a key Democrat in the City of New York," he said. Of course, this was absolute nonsense, I was neither, but this was Herb's way.

As a result of this event, I was invited to be a part of an informal advisory group for Rudy Giuliani's run for mayor of the City of New York. This group included many of the most fascinating people I have ever met, some of whom have become lifelong friends. Among the many activities were our Tuesday briefings, designed to inform and educate on all of the major issues facing the city. I joined Rudy and this amazing group for sessions with some intriguing people, experts in drugs, crime, homelessness, welfare, and many other areas, all working to inform Rudy and his team of the issues and challenges ahead. This was part of a quest to learn and form a strategy to rescue a city in serious danger, fully two years before the election would take place. It was a quest from the very beginning to develop a plan to solve the city's fundamental problems. I had a ringside seat, watching and participating with this gifted man and his team as they prepared to save New York City.

In 1990, *Time* magazine's cover appropriately declared New York "The Rotten Apple." It was a city with thousands of murders a year, more than one million people on welfare, and a budget deficit of close to $2 billion. Critically, a survey of New Yorkers suggested that, for the first time in memory, middle-class New Yorkers did not want to raise their children in the city, and if they could move, they would. Those of us on Rudy's unofficial committee knew that people lived, worked, and came to New York because it was a city of opportunity. New York captured the feeling people associated with passing the Statue of Liberty on the ships of the early twentieth-century immigration wave. New York could never be this place as long as people were not, and did not feel, safe. Crime and fear take away all possibilities.

People were scared, that was no surprise, but underlying the fear was an unstated assumption, in the government at the time, and the prevailing wisdom, that *the City of New York was not governable.* The problems were too vast, the crime and welfare problems deeply institutionalized. The best that people could hope for was a sort of "containment" of the problems, that the city would do its best to keep a lid on crime, and individuals should learn how to avoid becoming victims. As testimony to this attitude, ads regularly appeared in the subways showing people how not to fall victim to a crime. Think of it, promoting strategies that assumed a permanent state of lawlessness! The objective was to help people live with the state of the city, and there was a lot of evidence to back up this sentiment. Many had tried to improve conditions and had failed. The atmosphere hanging over the city was oppressive. As a longtime resident, I remember well how you looked over your shoulder as you walked to your apartment door.

The hidden agenda: "We need more than excuses and explanations; we need someone to fix the problem, or we're leaving!"

This desire held amongst the citizens was manifest in the statistics. Polls showed vast numbers of people were either leaving the city, or would do so and raise their children elsewhere if they could, a death knell for any metropolis. What was desired was a person to do something to really and truly fix the problem. The successful quest for the Mayoralty was a deep appreciation for this *hidden agenda*, and the instinctive response, often said by Mayor Giuliani, starting with his inaugural address,

"People created this problem, and people can fix the problem."

 ## Okay, Here's How

When you have arrived at the basic idea of your prospect's hidden agenda, it is important to encapsulate it in a simple, emotionally laden statement. This helps you and your entire team to integrate the spirit and emotional content that your prospect feels into all that you do. Spend time on this, work together as a team, and choose your words carefully. This key statement is your ticket to winning. There are essentially three components: *the subject, the emotional trigger,* and *the referent.*

The Subject

This is the company or organization in question and begins in the first person, *"I"* or *"we."* It is a personal or collective sentiment. For each type (want, need, or value), the statement begins:

> *I want...*
> *I need...*
> *I value the idea that...*

Emotional Trigger

This is the core emotional motivation at work (i.e., fear, ambition, longing, worry, enthusiasm) that reflects how the prospect is feeling.

Referent

This is the operative issue that gives rise to the emotion. It is what triggers the emotional core.

Using the three different types of hidden agendas, here are some examples of hidden agenda statements:

> **Want:** *I want people to recognize me for having created a financial services powerhouse.*

> **Need:** *We need to score a victory over Visa in the marketplace, and in doing so become famous for it...but we're not so sure we can.*

Values: *I value the idea that people created the problem, so people can fix the problem.*

Vive la "Priceless"

Several years after establishing the "Priceless" campaign in the United States, we pitched to MasterCard in France, which proved to be the ultimate torture test of the power of the hidden agenda. By this time, I was in charge of new business for McCann in Europe, the Middle East, and Africa. As the now-famous and highly successful "Priceless" campaign was taking the United States by storm, MasterCard's headquarters was keen to see it travel around the world. We quickly learned it wasn't going to be so easy.

As we launched our "foreign adventure," we discovered that with each individual pitch, market by market, we would find ourselves pitted against a rival for the business. Local marketing representatives, as you can imagine, were not eager to see their local programs and agency relationships upset by the American invasion of "Priceless" and McCann. We were confident, though, and thought we had a huge competitive advantage with "Priceless."

The French MasterCard client, icy cold to us at our initial briefing, announced that we were to pitch against a highly creative and acclaimed local agency. To add insult to injury, the client declared that the "Priceless" campaign (our campaign!) would be given to the other agency to work with as well, and each of us would develop versions of the campaign for the French market. May the best "Priceless" pitch win.

On the face of it, a contest with our campaign in the hands of a local favorite was a losing hand. I huddled with the management of our Paris office, and Gerard Charbit, the president of the Paris branch and a brilliant pitchman himself, made a keen observation. While the immediate clients, the local marketing executives, were against us, the managing director of MasterCard France would make the ultimate decision. Gerard did his homework on this individual, who was slated to be in the job less than a year, destined for a much bigger job in the company. Gerard reckoned that the only thing that could stop him from moving on to his big promotion was something going wrong in his current role. "We should make it our duty to ensure that nothing goes wrong for him," Gerard said. There was the answer. We were the experts on "Priceless," and getting the execution of a "Priceless" ad right was not easy. An agency that doesn't understand the nuances could easily get it wrong. It would look bad for him if a high-visibility campaign flopped in the French market. That was our pitch.

We knew from toiling for so many years with this idea that the art of creating effective "Priceless" advertising was a difficult one, requiring careful balance and finesse. So we based our stance on giving the managing director the best advice we could.

The hidden agenda: I need to be sure no mistakes are made that could cost me my promotion.

The resulting pitch: "Priceless" can go wrong, but we can make sure it's great. The *emotional trigger* was fear of disaster and the *referent* was the managing director's fabulous new job. Our pitch was effectively to protect his flanks by ensuring that "Priceless" in France would not only succeed but would become as famous and as beloved in the French market as it was in the United States. He decided hands down in our favor. *Voilà!*

My First Hidden Agenda

It was June of 1965. I was ten (little did I know then that I was destined for a life as a pitchman). For a variety of reasons, including getting shaken down on the way to school each day for my milk money (mobsters in training), I decided it was time for me to begin earning some money. My brother David had already gotten himself a paper route, but I was judged too young. I noticed that a number of boys in the neighborhood would borrow their fathers' lawnmowers and on Saturdays, for two whole dollars, mow the neighbors' lawns. I quickly did the math and realized that if I could get three, four, or maybe five customers, I could make a fortune. The problem, of course, was securing a lawnmower. So my first pitch was to my next-door neighbor, Wayne, to convince him what a marvelous idea it would be for the two of us to go into business together. Safe to say, his dad's lawnmower was secured, and while Wayne stood dutifully by the lawnmower at the foot of the driveway, I presented myself to the various gentlemen around the neighborhood as the answer to their lawn mowing dreams. Every single one sent me packing.

I decided to shift my focus to a target that I felt eminently more comfortable with and that I thought I could reach. So, rather than repeat running the gauntlet of the husbands, I targeted the wives, whom I would visit just after school. This time I prepared, creating a drawing and a name for my little company, which I called *Yankee Clipper*. Having been taught how to tie a bow tie by my grandfather a few years before, I donned my white Communion shirt and my little blue bowtie, and I knocked on the door of these very same houses. Only this time, presenting my widest smile, I thrust my little piece of paper in the lady of the house's hand and said, "Hi, my name is Kevin, the Yankee Clipper, and I'd like to mow your lawn, and half of what I make I'm going to give to the Veterans' Home in Babylon." I closed every sale. (And yes, I did give half to the VFW, ask my mother!)

And Now...

Pitching in an intimate setting involves groups that, by definition, share a common purpose and desire. Creating a following on a larger scale involves an audience that is very likely varied and complex. Now I'll share a great method of creating a following by identifying the hidden agenda they share.

REMEMBER THIS

Behind every decision there is a *hidden agenda*, the unspoken wants, needs, or values that reside in the hearts of your buyers. This hidden agenda is the true motivator behind every successful pitch. When you identify it and connect your strengths, beliefs, and ambitions to this hidden agenda, you win.

2

The Conceptual Target

. . . .

The *conceptual target* is a community of individuals bound by a common hidden agenda, with implications for what's really important to them and for how you invite them to follow you.

Why do some messages connect with an audience and others fail? Can it be as simple as this? *"I like what I hear"* or *"It is as if the message was meant for me."* The reason for this resonance is that the message connects with a hidden agenda *of the community.* Igniting your following through the power of the hidden agenda is best when you can develop a definition that stands as a universally held understanding of who your followers are and what is dear to them. More importantly, it crystallizes for you the hidden agenda that you must connect with in everything you say and do.

The *conceptual target* rests on the key principle that target audiences are not numbers, or age groupings, or functional descriptions. Nor are they laundry lists of characteristics. A conceptual target is simply a community of individuals who share common human truths. It is a highly evocative and stirring articulation of *what these people are about*, with enormous implications for what attracts them and how you might expect them to behave. One of my favorite conceptual targets, which arises out of the political arena, is the "soccer mom." The huge audience of women denoted by the term *soccer mom* is widely varied in where they live, how much they earn, and their lifestyles, but they are bound together by a sentiment that lies in their hearts. I have a conceptual target of people I call "growth aspirants." These are adventurers, spirited and forward-looking people who aspire to create something where nothing existed before.

Conceptual targeting is highly effective because it is based upon the principle that creating a following is a human endeavor, rooted not in facts and figures but in emotions, desires, and beliefs. This vital step provides a window on the "community" you seek to reach and on how you can connect with them. So, then, a critical component of creating a following is an inspired articulation of the conceptual target. My grasp of this concept was laid down very early in my career.

It's All About the *Who*

One of the many benefits of my years in the advertising business was the chance to meet dozens of extraordinary people. Undoubtedly, one of the most remarkable, confounding, and, at the same time, lovable people was Hank Seiden. Few were more certain of their convictions, or more unwavering in their beliefs about how to sell, than Hank. The agency he owned, a company called Hicks & Greist, merged with the New York office of Ketchum Advertising, and he became its leader. It is there we met.

Hank was a formidable character. A no-nonsense former creative director from the days when they threw T squares at account guys, Hank did not suffer fools. He could be brusque and dismissive, but also had a heart of gold. He had a big soft spot for me, and always gave me time, no matter what the circumstances. Hank was also, without a doubt, one of the funniest people I have ever worked with. As he was holding forth in his office one afternoon, reminding me for the thousandth time about the discipline and orderliness required to create an ad, the door of his office swung open and an elegant woman entered the room. She was simply radiant. "Good afternoon, young man," she greeted me. "Henry, I'm off to Bloomingdale's and then to meet Rachel. Don't forget we're meeting at 7:30 at the Abelow's. Now, don't be late." With a charming smile, she turned and left as swiftly and as regally as she had arrived. Now, I'd never heard *anybody* refer to the formidable Hank Seiden as Henry. Looking sheepish, shrugging his shoulders, and in a perfect Jackie Mason accent, Hank remarked, "You know...I believe in reincarnation, do you know why?" Taking the bait, of course, I asked why. He replied, "Because I'm coming back as Mrs. Henry Seiden!"

While he was one of the most amusing people in the business, Hank was also one of its wisest. "In business," he used to say, "you don't earn a nickel, you earn five pennies." He knew marketing was all about an idea, and there were no shortcuts to getting it. Only hard work, focus, and discipline would do. Hank wrote a book on the business called *Advertising Pure and Simple*. He believed that success was achieved through the basics, the *who, what,* and *how,* always in that order. He never wavered, gave in to fads, took shortcuts, or listened to anyone or anything that diverted him from the grit of creating a great pitch for us or for our clients. I think he went to the same school as Enid Merin, our door-to-door encyclopedia salesperson.

Hank believed things went wrong when people moved immediately to the *how*, that is, to the execution or the technique. He said, disdainfully, that it was because the *how* was the easy and fun part. He believed that these shortcut efforts always end in tears because they fail to do the very hard work that is necessary to understand intimately the individuals you are targeting, the *who*. Only after exhaustively turning over every potential bit of understanding of the target and arriving at a rich articulation of who these people are do you have permission to move to the *what* and the *how*. Great thinking, from a great man.

Creating a Following

I've read just about every Winston Churchill biography you can lay your hands on. I am sure many of you can remember one of this great statesman's most famous lines:

> *"We shall fight on the beaches, we shall fight on the landing grounds, we shall fight in the fields and in the streets, we shall fight in the hills; we shall never surrender..."*

I recall reading that when Churchill wrote his speech, he remarked that he was not imposing this idea upon the British people but rather articulating something that they all felt collectively in their hearts. All he was doing was crystallizing and sharing a declaration they already believed. He effectively created a following by igniting a feeling held in the hearts of the British people.

Creating a following is not "imposition." It is what I call *"buoyancy."* Buoyancy is a phenomenon whereby, as a leader of a following, you "float," because the people in the community you have inspired believe that you should. They believe in you, support you, celebrate your strengths, and shore up your weaknesses, all because you understand and connect with what lies in their hearts. Creating a following is rooted in a fundamental understanding of your audience's collective hidden agenda and in an ability to crystallize that agenda into a common definition that binds them as one.

Creating a following is somewhat more complex than pitching to a small group of five or six. By definition, the larger the group of people, the higher the likelihood that they will differ widely by age and income or in functional ways of describing and targeting them. A brilliant way to describe a large audience (your following) as a common community rooted in a collective hidden agenda that you can ignite, can be found in what is called a *conceptual target.*

The Evolution of Targeting

Careful targeting has always been a mainstay in the marketing and advertising fields, and in the political arena as well. Many of us in marketing learned about the notion of the "target audience," the group to whom we would direct our marketing efforts. It was invariably defined in functional terms and usually by demographic, for example, males aged twenty-five to fifty-four, teens from sixteen to eighteen, women thirty-five to fifty-four, and so on. This clear delineation drove all we did, from shaping the messaging to executing it to delivering it via different media. With an ever-increasing competitive environment pressuring marketers and agencies alike, new methods of understanding target audiences developed. The target audience description would be given an additional layer of information, called *psychographics*. This additional dimension, which aimed to understand the psychological nature common to the group, would be added to the demographic description, in a list format. Looking back, target audience descriptions were generally fairly lengthy and filled with bits and pieces of information. Not a process that inspires. Nor was it one that lent itself to creating a larger aggregate. The functional differences among the individuals was simply too vast for there to be a meaningful common ground.

The Origins of Conceptual Targeting

The origins of pinpointing with clarity and intensity the emotions and deeply held desires of a community of like-minded people can be found in politics of the latter twentieth century. In the spring of 1979, a man by the name of Joe Plummer put forward to his colleague Richard Wirthlin, a renowned pollster, the idea that a very different strategic method could help a former actor-turned-governor become president. I first met Joe, a bighearted and gregarious man, at McCann. He was a senior strategic planner working on multinational accounts like Nestlé and Coca-Cola. He is now a professor of global marketing at Columbia University. An optimist with a booming voice that could knock you across the room, Joe played a role in two of the most important American political campaigns in recent memory, but his humble manner is such that one literally has to drag his enormous contributions out of him. I managed to do so.

Joe was invited to help create political strategy for Ronald Reagan, then a successful governor but a somewhat dubious presidential candidate. The political polling process took its usual turn, identifying all of the traditional voter segments that would be needed to secure a win. Vitally important but disparate demographics included large portions of the white male voting bloc, among them older Southern, urban working-class, and suburban conservative voters. On the face of it, the disparate demographic descriptions made it difficult to find any ground for common campaign appeal. Joe directed the people undertaking the polling to come back with attitudinal elements that were common to these groups. He said, "I thought that there must be some kind of emotional sentiment all these men had in their hearts that irrespective of where they lived, what they did, or even how they previously voted, could be uncovered and leveraged in campaign communication." Joe theorized that a mass constituency made up of disparate parts could be held together by a deeply held emotional sentiment, a conceptual target.

When the results came in, two key things emerged. The first was the profound sense of alienation among all of these men. They felt that no one was paying attention. Joe commented, "It was as if their voice and their contributions simply didn't count anymore." The second thing they had in common was a feeling that the country, once a great and powerful nation, had become weak and had lost its sway to other powers in the world, financially to the Japanese and militarily to the Soviet Union.

Joe crystallized the conceptual target as "angry white guys." This galvanized the thinking of the campaign, linking these men together as a "community" with a common value system and set of concerns, all of which he realized could be tied to

46

the strengths of Ronald Reagan and his perceived abilities as a leader. The confident tone struck by the resulting campaign of making America strong again resonated among this conceptual target. The campaign, which included a now-famous television commercial, "Morning in America," was an uplifting story of what America could become, which resonated at the core of how the conceptual target felt and what they longed for. They voted overwhelmingly for a former actor to become the fortieth president of the United States.

Soccer Moms

Joe's strategic abilities would be drawn on once again, this time on the opposite side of the political spectrum, to assist Bill Clinton's campaign for the presidency. This time it was not men but women who were the subject of the debate. In a similar way, the disparate demography gave way to a powerfully insightful observation about women with children, whether they lived in Greenwich, Connecticut, or Duluth, Minnesota.

Many of America's women were leading hectic lives, shuttling the kids to school, athletic activities, and a host of after-school pursuits while maintaining a household, and often working outside the home as well. Their huge struggle, by any standard, was set against the backdrop of an economy in shambles and record-breaking deficits that made it seem to these women that no matter how hard they tried, they were going backward. To these women, it seemed as if they struggled alone, with an unsympathetic government mortgaging the country's future. Their biggest concern, though, was not their own plight but their belief that, for the first time in recent memory, their children's lives would not be better than theirs, and in fact they would likely be worse. The now-famous conceptual target of "soccer moms" became a powerful label for this group of important voters. Bill Clinton's message resonated with individuals who felt that they were alone in their struggle. Clinton's identity as the "Boy from Hope" offered these women and others in the country a sense that he, through his empathy and youthful vigor, could dismantle old-style politics and embrace the newly emerging technological revolution to their benefit and to the benefit of their children. Soccer moms made a disproportionate contribution in securing Bill Clinton's place as the forty-second president of the United States.

From my perspective, the power of Joe and his colleagues' work in defining the notion of conceptual targeting was that they were able to ladder to a single emotional mindset among a demographically disparate group of people. They were able to craft a single emotional definition that could be tapped to create a following. It was a remarkable accomplishment from an even more remarkable fellow, my good friend Joe.

Today's Relevance

What Joe and his colleagues pioneered was a means of defining a community of individuals who share an emotional like-mindedness. The urge to congregate with like-minded people is ageless. Abraham Maslow, an American professor of psychology, told us that after the vital needs of shelter and sustenance were provided for, a human being's next most important need was to belong. This is the fundamental human desire to have relationships, to be understood and accepted. It is the emotional security that is found in being appreciated and wanted, in loving and being loved.

We have observed how, over millennia, humans have evolved and survived by banding together. Long ago they came together as tribes. These affinity groups were bound together in a bid for survival, survival against every known threat, including the elements, animals, and other tribes. People's survival depended on collective action and unity, expressed through a shared value system, a set of deeply held beliefs, practices, customs, and aspirations.

These values were ultimately made iconic, expressed in symbols such as tartans, coats of arms, and indeed the flags of nations. Kings have come and gone, and so have empires and dynasties, but the desire and need to express a collective set of closely held values has endured. I like to call them *citizenships*. But something dramatic has happened: the ultimate democratization. Thanks to the power of today's digital technology, these citizenships have taken on a new quality. They are now vast and borderless, united by common value systems and shared beliefs but untethered by geography. Reaching these citizenships, and creating a following among them, requires understanding the hidden agenda they hold in common, the collective desire they share, however far-flung or varied in composition the individuals may be. A common emotional desire will bind them together and, if you connect to it, will bind them to you.

Okay, Here's How…

With all that you know about the individuals in your audience and their hidden agendas, get creative. What kind of emotional label can you create that telegraphs in a second how these individuals are connected? The best conceptual target descriptors are those that can be summarized in no more than three words. For example, when determining the conceptual target for an over-the-counter medication marketer, our advertising team discovered that the individual in the household most concerned with family health issues was the mother. For us, she was the "chief medical officer." As women increasingly took roles outside the home in the business world, they delegated many of their tasks to others, but the one role they universally felt could never be compromised or relinquished was seeing to the health of each and every member of the family.

For one of our private banking clients whose targets were entrepreneurial businesspeople, we coined a conceptual target called the "self-made visionary." Nothing was given to these individuals; they started at the bottom with nothing more than their ambitions and their wits. No silver spoon in the mouth for these people. They were self-made successes with the vision to see possibilities and the guts to make them happen.

When writing a conceptual target definition, you are not creating a technical descriptor. What you are writing is by definition a creative expression, an idea that encapsulates the target in emotional terms. It is value system–based, which is why it can contain so many disparate functional groups as part of its community. Here are some questions to consider when writing a conceptual target:

1. What kinds of people belong to this group? What kinds of lives do they lead?
2. What do they seek, what keeps them up at night?
3. What are their hopes and aspirations?

And when you arrive at a conceptual target description, ask yourself:

4. Does my conceptual target description incorporate all the functional descriptors of the individual groups that comprise it?
5. Does it have emotional content? Can I feel it?
6. Does it ring true?
7. Does it strike at the heart of the hidden agenda I have arrived at?

The following sections illustrate a few of my favorite examples of strong conceptual target descriptions.

Marriott: The Road Warrior

When we pitched for the Marriott International business (I'll give you the whole story shortly), we had stacks of information on the demographic and psychographic characteristics of the Marriott Hotel audience. The real task was to articulate a highly evocative conceptual target that would reflect the spirit of the many thousands of individuals who stayed at Marriott hotels around the country and indeed across the world. It was very common at the time, and perhaps it is even today, when thinking about business targets, to describe them in stratospheric terms. Captains of industry, people at the seat of power, and achievers all conjure up imagery of private jets, boardrooms, and corridors of power.

The work of the team showed a very different picture. The vast mosaic of individuals traveling relentlessly from appointment to appointment were genuine, hard-working individuals who, oftentimes unnoticed, spent many days away from their homes and families, giving themselves for the benefit of their companies. This honorable bedrock of the business world, whether junior salespeople or CEOs, were all out there "sell-ing," and all shared a noble value system. They were honor-able people doing honorable work, selling and winning for the people who matter most: their companies and their families.

The hidden agenda of Marriott guests captured the spirit of people willing to endure sacrifices to succeed:

"We want to succeed for our families and companies and will not give up in doing so."

We called the conceptual target for these exceptional folks "road warriors." As a means of bringing life to this conceptual target description, Peter Kim, our vice-chairman, paused in presenting his careful description of these folks, produced a book of plays, and described the soul of the "road warrior" by reading:

Nobody dast blame this man . . . Willy was a salesman. And for a salesman, there's no rock bottom to life. He don't put a nut to a bolt. He don't tell you the law or medicine. He's a man way out there in the blue riding on a smile and a shoeshine.
                    Death of a Salesman, *Arthur Miller*

Fabulous.

MasterCard: Good Revolvers

The most difficult enemy in the MasterCard pitch was not any of the twenty agencies we were up against, it was the excruciat-ing forces of parity. In a way, that was the magic. The key to success would be found not in a statistic or a fact or in some sort of superiority claim but in human insight. We struggled with many things in developing the MasterCard pitch, the first being an understanding of the community that comprised the MasterCard target audience. Finding some difference between the audience demographics of Visa and MasterCard was virtually impossible. The audiences were just too similar.

In the course of studying the problem, the strategic trinity of Eric Einhorn, Suresh Nair, and Nat Puccio arrived at a breakthrough definition based upon emotional commonalities among card users, most importantly identifying those qualities that resonated with the DNA of the MasterCard brand. Common to all these individuals, irrespective of demographics, was a hidden agenda of *wanting to provide the very best for the people that they loved.* This insight was made even more powerful as a consequence of a profound shift in societal values toward those that were more inner-directed. The further magic was that all of this connected to the very essence of the MasterCard brand. The conceptual target of people "buying good things, for good reasons, for good people" was called the "good revolver" (a "revolver," in credit card parlance, is a person who does not pay the balance in full but does so in monthly installments). As our ad team spoke with literally dozens of credit card holders, it became clear that, while they "revolved" or rolled over a balance, all felt the same way. Their purchases were made for good reasons, for the people they loved. As my mother, clearly one of these people, pointed out when asked how she single-handedly managed to raise a house full of children with all the challenges life threw at her, replied, "Well, lots of hard work, perseverance, patience, a bit of luck, and my credit cards!" With the strategic work to identify the target done, we looked back to put it in hidden agenda terms, uncovering what was in the heart of the MasterCard conceptual target:

THE HIDDEN AGENDA

The hidden agenda: We're not reckless free spenders, we just want a good life for the people we care about.

One very early morning, with but a few weeks left until the pitch, my friend and a brilliant Creative Director named Jonathan Cranin rang me, and our conversation went something like this:

"I think I've got something."

"OK, I'll be right down."

"Ah, let's do it later. Never mind."

"You're killing me, I'm coming down."

I entered his office, and there, on the white screen on his computer was a simple line.

There are some things money can't buy. For everything else there's MasterCard.

"Oh, my God, we've won the business!"

Within a few days, this inspirational thought was shared with several people, including a gifted creative team, Joyce King Thomas and Jeroen Bours. Their objective: create a campaign idea from Jonathan's seminal thought. Very soon thereafter, we met to see what had developed. In her own gentle yet riveting style, Joyce explained that there were things in life you simply could not put a price on and presented an idea the world now knows as *Priceless*. The win, and the global following it created, came because our clients and their customers alike were enchanted by a simple yet fundamental human truth held among a community of like-minded people who were ignited by our commitment to them and their aspirations.

At the core of this humble brand was a conceptual target of individuals who had like values and a shared ambition, who agreed that MasterCard stood for more than the purchases it afforded. It was this image that stood at the heart of the hidden agenda for the MasterCard brand. In short: good people buying good things for good reasons. We called our conceptual target—generous, hard-working, and thoughtful people—"good revolvers," and these were the people who would embrace the little piece of plastic as theirs because it reflected their own deeply held values.

Ericsson: Everyday Heroes

Recently, one of my clients was invited to contend for the worldwide communications business of the technology giant Ericsson. Looking closely at the company, we were awed by the huge global presence literally wiring up the planet in some hundred and fifty countries. My client, meeting with me after the briefing, was struck by how different the company was from what they had been expecting. They went in expecting highly analytical, task-oriented people, the type you might find in a global technology company, doing the heavy lifting of wiring up the world. Instead, they found warm, engaging people who spoke more about Ericsson's role in the world than its technological prowess. After the briefing meeting came the exhaustive research on what the company actually does. Buried in a little internal brochure was a sort of company mission. It said that the people of Ericsson were in virtually every country in the world, from major metropolitan centers to remote places where nearly no one goes. The company, it went on, was doing "important work to better people's lives around the world." The team could sense, however, that the people at Ericsson felt that this vital work of building communications infrastructure was, while maybe not so glamorous, absolutely essential to human development, though their efforts were going unnoticed. The hidden agenda:

We want to be appropriately recognized for making a difference in the lives of people around the world because of what our business does.

That was it. It was now clear that Ericsson could step out of the shadows and share its collective pride for the important work it was doing to help communities prosper. Ericsson's conceptual target: "the everyday hero."

I left the group to develop the presentation, returning some weeks later, about five days before the pitch. I entered their "war room," with its walls papered with charts, graphs, and white sheets with lots of scribbling; on individual white cards tacked on the wall were six key concepts. Among them was a simple idea: "Creating Everyday Miracles." I turned to the group and reminded them of the conceptual target we'd established. It was clear. This was the unmistakable recommendation, and my client won the business unanimously.

This shows not only how useful the conceptual target can be in defining a community of followers but also demonstrates its value as a screening criterion for judging the means by which you will connect with your target. Without this conceptual target framework, what would be the criteria for selecting among the six different concepts created to connect with Ericsson's internal and external followers? Based upon the written technical brief, it's likely that the "Everyday Miracles" concept would not have been chosen, and a less-than-optimal connection with internal and external Ericsson followers would have been made. It was also evidence that a conceptual target isn't ethereal, but a galvanizing idea that gives purpose to the process of connecting with your following.

And Now...

With the hidden agenda now defined and its larger constituency tool, the conceptual target, identified, the question now is, How do you uncover the hidden agenda? How do you find it even if you can't meet your audience face to face? How do you uncover the unspoken, visceral, emotional desire that lies in their hearts? Elementary, my dear readers...

REMEMBER THIS

The *conceptual target* is a tool that identifies your audience in terms of its *hidden agenda.* It is the crystallization of a community of individuals who share common human truths. The conceptual target is a highly evocative and stirring articulation of *what these people are about,* and has enormous implications for what attracts them and how you will pitch to them.

3

Uncovering the Hidden Agenda

. . . .

Unlocking the hidden agenda requires you to get close to your prospect and to listen carefully to read the emotional subject at hand. It means asking questions that open a window to your audience's emotional motivation.

One of my boyhood heroes was my Uncle Don. He wasn't actually an uncle by blood, but was my mother and father's best friend. His wife, Aunt Betty, looked exactly like Glinda the Good Witch in *The Wizard of Oz*. I loved them. Uncle Don was a cop, and eventually he went from humble beginnings as a foot patrolman to a gold shield homicide detective in Nassau County, New York. I would sit entranced when he visited as he told stories of chasing down robbers (literally) and, of course, my favorite, questioning his suspects. "One thing you can count on is nothing is as it seems from the start. Only when you do a bit of digging can you reveal what is really going down. You've got to be one part cop, two parts priest, and five parts shrink," he observed. Well, our targets are hardly wrongdoers, but just as Uncle Don doesn't think strictly like a cop when he is probing for the truth, nor should we think only as business-people when approaching the search for the hidden agenda.

Raise Your Emotional Antennae

The search for the hidden agenda is the search for desire. It is rarely in evidence. You will need to put on special antennae to receive these signals. There is no trickery or hidden persuasion in finding your audience's hidden agenda. What is required is emotional insight, human sensitivity, thoughtfulness, empathy, and *very* good listening skills. These can be applied in a scientific approach that may require you to unlearn some of your previous ways and means of pitching.

The search for the hidden agenda will sometimes take place under circumstances where you have access to your audience, but in some cases, access may be restricted or filtered. The latter is, of course, very challenging, but it is still possible to unearth the hidden agenda at work. Let's begin with the prospect that is available to you in advance of the presentation itself.

A Little Help . . . Please

I once led a pitch for a contact lens brand from Johnson & Johnson. Each contender was given a single meeting prior to the pitch. We drew the short straw and were the last ones to meet the marketing head of this challenged company. Our prospect was clearly a senior guy, and from what I could detect, he was a person who had been around. As soon as we got into the room, I could sense he was distracted. It was very subtle, but it was apparent to me that something about all of this made him very uncomfortable. After some questions to get the ball rolling, I asked, "So, how do you feel about this process?" He lit up. "I'd rather have root canal."

After a number of questions, I finally asked, "What is it about this that makes you crazy?" He replied emphatically, "If I have one more kid take thirty minutes to tell me how screwed up my business is, I swear I'll commit homicide!"

Clearly, in his mind this kind of questioning was not productive. Moreover, I could see a veteran like him would be kind of embarrassed to have well-meaning "youngsters" grill him on the issues. Not wanting this to take place, I could see that what this man was looking for was purposeful people like him who looked at the glass as half full. He was a no-nonsense man who responded to those who looked for solutions. (This practice is what I call reading the room: You detect what is happening, and then shift the dialogue accordingly.) We proceeded to probe all of what we called his strategic assets, and the tempo and enthusiasm of the session went onto overdrive.

I am pleased to say we did go on to win the business.. Our theme would be based on unbridled optimism and possibility (I seem to recall we dubbed it the *"Possibility Agenda"*) where we dwelled on nothing about the problem and everything about the possibilities. When later I asked him why we got the business, his reply was, "You listened."

Invitation Versus Interrogation

First, and I know this sounds obvious, get as close to your prospect as you can. Spend as much time as the prospect will allow.

I am utterly amazed at how often a group that is pursuing a deal or an account does not meet informally with the prospective audience before the formal presentation. Madness! But when you do meet, make it an experience your prospect will enjoy, not an interrogation they will dread. There are four key steps in the process, and these encompass both the lead-up and the actual meeting with your prospective buyer:

1. Prepare: The brief is not the brief.
2. Be receptive.
3. Think like a shrink.
4. Listen in the right way.
5. Ask the right questions.

Let's look at these steps more closely.

1. Prepare: The brief is not the brief.

As a pitch is crafted, we initially confront functional realities. These might include a sagging brand, an organization that needs restructuring, and the like. Dealing with these realities is, of course, the task. The task, however, is only one element in the solution. In advance of a pitch, the prospect generally issues some kind of "brief." It could come in the form of a simple letter or e-mail that includes a short description of what you should prepare or the problem to be addressed. You might, on the other hand, receive a tight prescription of what you are to prepare, with an exhaustive collection of supporting materials.

I've watched dozens of companies pitch amazing solutions to the brief, only to scratch their heads and ask how on earth they could have lost. What is critical is not what's in the brief functionally, but what lies in the heart of your prospect, and how that will be central to your response. No matter what form the brief takes and no matter what the brief articulates, *this is not the real desire at work and the all-important hidden agenda you must pitch to.* The hidden agenda is the basis upon which the pitch will *really* be decided. The brief must be answered, of course, but your answer to this brief must be made within the context of the buyer's hidden agenda.

Use secondary information and other homework to prepare an understanding of your buyer, then discuss and establish your hypothesis for the hidden agenda. I like this technique because it places the team in a hidden agenda–search mindset before meeting with the buyer. It allows the time during the meeting to be spent following lines of questioning and filtering what you hear in a less technical context.

2. Be Receptive.

Imagine meeting someone for the first time. You don't declare formally, "I would like to make a friendship. It will be based on the following criteria." Instead, you chat and, through human insight, find some common ground. Pitching is an entirely human endeavor. You must get close to your prospect not just physically, but emotionally. I am astounded by how many companies, after receiving a brief, spend little or no time with the client until the day they walk into the boardroom. This means that a sense of the prospect's profile, an understanding of the hidden agenda, and then a recommendation based on that agenda needs to take place in the course of three hours. Impossible.

Your first encounter prior to a formal presentation is a vitally important element in uncovering the hidden agenda. Many of these sessions are formal briefing meetings, where you have an opportunity to respond, or are scheduled question-and-answer sessions once the brief has been issued. In either case, the question-and-answer session is *your meeting*. This is your opportunity to carefully control events and to search for the hidden agenda at work. There is no step more important in the process than this.

The question-and-answer session can be very intimidating for a person at the other end of the query. It turns the tables, with your buyers on the receiving end of a meeting they don't control. This is very uncomfortable. One client told me after we had won the pitch and we got to know one another that it felt like an interrogation. Many "pursuers" see the Q & A session as an opportunity to ask smart questions. This is a disaster in the making. The objective is to not to show off but to get the prospect to reveal the things you need to know. It is *not* about you.

Getting to the hidden agenda requires you to focus on the prospect and to put them at ease. My Uncle Don, the detective, observed, "To get to the heart of things, I make them as comfortable as possible. No one is going to share anything with someone they are afraid of. If they are intimidated, they'll say anything just to make you go away." I use the term "interview" when I think or talk about these meetings. It puts a completely different hue on the experience, moving the prospect from "on the spot" to "in the spotlight." It's flattering, and transitions the experience from an investigation to a celebration of the prospect's company. Your prospect will feel good, and will be more likely to relax and let you in. An interrogation is meant to scrutinize, an interview is meant to celebrate.

When you listen, try to be conscious about shifting the attention away from yourself. Focus on the prospect and open yourself up, using good body language: palms up, no crossing of arms or legs. Much has been written about this fascinating and highly relevant subject. People communicate in a "whole" manner through speech, with their eyes, and with tone and inflection. They speak with their bodies, too. As Uncle Don remarks, "You can see right away that what they're saying and how they're acting are two different things." Similarly, you can see when the prospect is animated and all feels in sync that you are on to something.

There are obvious positive signals, like open arms, palms up for optimism and confidence, as well as defensive signals like crossed arms and rapid eye movements. I tend to step back and take a whole view of prospective clients to see how relaxed or tense they are. I watch when they are answering questions and moments when they "light up," both physically and in speech patterns. Emotions are at work. This is where you need to probe, because this is the emotional vein to mine that will lead you to their desire. Watch for it, and when you do, direct a laddering of questions down this path.

Sit up and lean forward. As they speak, nod and acknowledge what you are hearing. At key pauses, most people will fill the space with what they want to say. Instead, paraphrase what the prospective clients have said and feed back to them what you have heard. It will let them know you care and it will give them the encouragement to *tell you more*.

3. Think like a shrink.

Every pursuit is about the audience's emotion, but this emotion will not be immediately visible. There are social conventions, political considerations, and an inherent vulnerability that go with admitting the underlying motivation that a person has in her heart. Remove the "professional practitioner" hat and instead become a psychotherapist. This change in perspective affects how you look at and approach the entire process, in both the questions you ask and the conclusions you draw. Observe carefully how questions are answered, especially the intensity around a subject.

Imagine that a team wishing to be retained goes to visit a prospective client. They all file into the conference room, with its usual coffee carafes, croissants, and fruit at the ready. A few pleasantries are exchanged and the team leader asks, "So what are you hoping to see from us in our next meeting?" Imagine that the prospect replies, "I'm hoping you will tell me how to do all of this, because I have absolutely *no* idea, and I'm terrified that everybody will find out!" Now, this may be the reason for the pitch but you can bet you'll never hear it stated quite like that! The feeling is there, though, in the prospect's heart, and the team that finds, unlocks, and attaches to it resonantly will win.

Before you go to your first meeting, or briefing, you must do your homework. Ask yourself:

Who is this person?
What can I learn about whom they are and what makes them tick?
What kind of personality profile are they?

These questions will determine how the prospect thinks and feels and will guide you in the approach you'll take to revealing the hidden agenda. When you get to know your audience prior to the meeting, you will be able to operate on a deeper plane. Your ability to observe and question your prospect will have a deeper and more meaningful context. So, do your homework and create a composite picture of the person and what makes them tick.

4. Listen in the right way.

Our new age increasingly supports the importance of the "outbound" message, with YouTube, blogging, and the like becoming ever more popular. This self-expression is wonderful in so many ways, but it leads one to ask: With all this talking, is anyone listening? In my experience, many see pitching as the "gift of gab." I think the best pitch person is one who is an incredibly insightful listener. We know how to speak. We're taught our native tongue, we add other languages, we take speech courses and elocution lessons, but how many of us have ever taken a course in listening? My mother maintains that I was inoculated with a phonograph needle. Guilty as charged. I was always yapping. Once in business, though, I realized I was surrounded by very bright people who spoke more than I did, and I remembered that my grandmother used to say, "It's the smart one who stays quiet." She was right. Sitting back allowed me to listen carefully to what was being said, consider my thoughts, and then when I spoke, to say something that resonated with the group.

Good listening skills will not only allow you to grasp the core of what your prospect is trying to convey, but you'll be able to see, as if you're wearing x-ray glasses, the desire locked inside the speaker's hidden agenda. Good listening, in my view, is an act of generosity. When you listen, you are putting the speaker's interests ahead of your own. The speaker is fulfilling a need by expressing something to you. Listening ensures that you come to know exactly what your prospect is attempting to convey, which tells them you care.

Look for clues about the personality profile of the prospect; this is their orientation and the way they look at things. (We'll look at this closely in Chapter 4, "Your Core.") Understanding the prospect will help you to filter his responses according to the way he sees the world, as dictated by his personality orientation. Acknowledge and paraphrase, giving your buyer the indication that it's his time to speak and share, and that you are receptive and supportive. The more comfortable he feels, the deeper and more candid he will be.

Of all the people in your organization, there are no doubt some who have highly defined intuition. Bring one or more of these "clairvoyants" with you to your meetings. They should be among your briefing team from the start. (On my teams, it was always me.) While others will be preoccupied with the task at hand and other "professional" issues, a person gifted with deep empathy will be focused on the underlying emotional issues at work. It's like having someone there with emotional "x-ray vision." This is where the magic of profiling comes in. If you do your homework ahead of time, you can ensure that you have a team member who is highly compatible with the prospect in the room. The two will relate well to one another, and your simpatico team member will aid in making the prospect feel comfortable and at ease in speaking the "language" he is comfortable with. Having a people-oriented person in the room with you allows you to carefully observe the dialogue from a purely human perspective. The empathetic team member can ensure that—while others are asking more functional questions—issues of a human interest nature are also explored.

5. Ask the right questions.

My mother used to say, if you ask a silly question, you get a silly answer. So, in this spirit, if you ask functional questions, you'll get functional answers. If your questions are more intuitive or emotional, you are on your way to revealing the hidden agenda. Include, of course, questions about the rational side of issues and those related to the business, but also ask questions that invite the prospect to express her views, feelings, and instincts. As you listen, don't write like a courtroom stenographer. Allow the facts to assemble into an overall theme of what the prospect is feeling and the idea she is trying to convey. The answers will reveal the elements of the hidden agenda, but only if you ask the kinds of questions that elicit an emotional response.

Briefing meetings all too often get down to brass tacks, with a focus on the task at hand. The "background" or "situation analysis," in my view, is the most essential part of the process, for it is there that the hidden agenda lurks. This is where the real desire will be found, and this is the discussion where you are most likely to discover the emotional desires of your buyer. It is at this stage in the process that the prospect finds themselves *in a state of unmet desire.*

In the briefing process, invite your prospect to elaborate on the situation. Make sure they expresses their opinions (feelings) about it. Do they see in the company's current circumstances an opportunity or a threat? A glass half empty or a glass half full? Here are some questions that will draw out the responses you're looking for:

I am intrigued by the current environment your company is in. Tell us more.

What are your instincts telling you?

Are there any parallels to this situation?

What is the biggest opportunity arising from this circumstance?

How do you think the company is feeling about it all?

As you probe effectively, a hidden agenda will begin to emerge. To help the process along, you can begin by posing questions that trigger a response in any one of the three hidden agenda states, *wants*, *needs*, and *values*, that we identified earlier.

Want

These types of future-forward questions draw out a confident prospect who has his eye on the future.

> *If you had to write a corporate dream, what would it be?*
> *What frustrates you about the perceptions of your company in the marketplace?*

Need

These questions will spark your prospect to express what concerns her:

> *What keeps you up at night?*
> *What stands in your way?*
> *What might set your plans back?*

Values

These questions will ignite a buyer whose self and company are guided by a sense of purpose based on a value system:

> *Do you believe there is a common value system in your company?*
> *How much do you think these beliefs will drive your solution?*
> *What would you say is your company's noble calling?*

As you probe these three hidden agenda states, one will emerge as most prominent. The prominent state will become clear by the amount of time that the prospect spends on the subject and the "lighting up" he does. If you're watching, you can't miss it. When you see this happening, move on to "laddering."

Laddering

The laddering technique can guide you in zeroing in on your buyer's hidden agenda. To understand this method and its importance, here's a little analogy: Communicating is like a moment in *Star Trek*, when Scotty beams people all over the place. First, he disassembles the person, then he sends him through space, then he reassembles him someplace else. As people communicate with you, what comes at you are all the pieces. It is for you to "assemble" them and draw an emotional picture.

Because the hidden agenda is the deep-rooted, visceral, and emotional reason behind the purchase or hiring decision, it's not going to be plainly in sight. It is invariably unstated. People themselves often do not realize with clarity where these desires lie, or the extent of their motivating power, and even if they do, societal norms are far too strong for these desires ever to be vocalized. *Laddering* is an excellent method of revealing these elements. It involves a connected series of questions that probe ever deeper into each response. When people are speaking, they tend to communicate in layers:

- Facts, anecdotes, stories
- The core idea or message
- The underlying emotion and desires at the heart

Laddering is a long-established technique in clinical psychology, and provides a means to understanding people's inner values and motivations. For a particular line of discussion, laddering is the formation of a "chain" of questions and replies that follow a path toward the essential core of how a person feels and her core motive. It gets behind the initial surface response to a question. This is why, to get to the true desire, you have to dig deep. In laddering, once you have "struck a vein," you stay on this line of questioning, asking "why" or related questions to probe more deeply for each response in a single line of thinking. The series of questions will take you deeper and deeper into the meaningful root of how the person feels. For example, here again is the line of questioning we followed in the Johnson & Johnson experience discussed earlier. You can see how the laddering moves the client from a generalized state to one where the elements of the hidden agenda unfold.

Q: *Are the Q & A sessions useful from your vantage point?*
A: Well, it's a necessary process to get the best result.

Q: *How do you feel about the process itself?*
A: I'd rather have root canal.

Q: *What is it about this that makes you crazy?*
A: If I have one more kid take thirty minutes to tell me how screwed up my business is, I swear I'll commit homicide!

Once we got to this moment, we all shared a laugh, but right then and there we knew to shift our line of discussion straight to the "glass half full" side of the equation, the side where we emphasized positive opportunities and how he and the brand could succeed. So when you are at the starting point, more often than not prospects will answer functionally. By following a laddered, emotional path, you create a chain that leads you to a more profound emotional core.

If You Can't Be There

Many tell me they often face circumstances where they will not have contact with the ultimate decision maker until the presentation, and if they do, it is for a very brief time. There is no denying that this makes the process very difficult indeed. But all is not lost! Remember, uncovering the hidden agenda is detective work involving not only witnesses and potential suspects, but also painstaking collection of clues and physical evidence.

"There's Gold in Them Thar Hills!" If you are unable to spend quality time with your audience, you need to rely on other sources to give you clues. This is real detective work. However, thanks to the ample availability of information about companies, it is possible to derive a hidden agenda from the things the company publishes about its business. Here's a little trick. Put two annual report letters side by side, and read the tone and style and value systems that the company communicated in their letters. This will tell you a great deal about the cultural underpinnings of the company. The material you can find on the Internet, in speeches, company brochures, and the secondary material that washes over the Internet, as well as the internal literature and the brief that the client gives you, are more important than ever. These texts may be the only thing you have that offer you vital clues.

There are a few other techniques that also can be useful:

1. Social media

There is an enormous amount of professional and personal information on the web. It is entirely possible (and advisable) to assemble a dossier on your buyer(s) from a deep dive online. We can learn a great deal about buyers, who they are and what kinds of lives they lead, through sites like LinkedIn and Facebook. Be thorough and check your facts, though, because anyone can enter information in the cloud. You've got to be sure of what's credible and what's not.

2. General secondary information

We are very lucky indeed. We live in a world where the democratization of information has given us unprecedented access to data of all kinds, including personal details. This material includes internal business communications, published articles, and the opinions of analysts and pundits.

I actually don't like the term "secondary," as it does not do justice to the richness of hidden agenda material that can be found. You can begin to create a mosaic of a person's career by looking at what is associated with him on the web. Reviewing it all can really give you a sense of his state of mind. Articles and blogs written by your prospect, or people close to the company, will be a rich treasure of insight and hidden agenda fodder.

Find out what is written about your prospect's company and the individuals you are pitching to. Look at the chatter about them around the Internet. The good news is that this information is out there and it's very robust. In a lot of cases, others have done the digging for you, offering their opinions, so it's only for you to see the pattern and interpret. *But I cannot reiterate strongly enough the importance of selecting the information carefully from credible sources and vetting it for reliability.*

3. Internal material

You may be inundated with material from your prospect, intended to help you prepare for your presentation. This material is inevitably about the company's externals, the circumstances it faces. It is rare that you are given a window inside the company or information about its value system and inner workings. Ask for material employees might see, like a new employee welcome pack, key messages from the CEO, and the like. These hold wonderful clues. As I described earlier, when my team won the Ericsson account, we'd found the clue to the hidden agenda inside an employee newsletter. Clients are often delighted when you express interest in probing inside their organizations to better understand their market position and their opportunities.

Visit downstream, especially the salespeople and others on the service "coal face," that is, the front line. This is where reality lives and where you learn the unvarnished truth; with it comes huge clues to the hidden agenda. Frustration or excitement will be manifest in those who are charged with getting the job done.

4. Six degrees of separation

It's often been said that there are no more than six people between you and anyone on the planet, however distantly "related" the other person may seem. Connecting to those in proximity to your prospect may provide an insider's view of the emotional makeup of your prospect and an unbridled look at the emotional triggers at work. I believe strongly in the notion of *contact strategy*, fanning out into the community of your prospect and linking from contact to contact to get as close to the inner circle as you can. This is where intimacy of observation will be found and vital unfiltered information gleaned about the hidden agenda at work.

5. Kids say the funniest things

I recently asked a group of business development people how many of them spent time with the most junior person on the prospect team. No hands went up. I always asked to see those junior people; not only is it a happy surprise for them, but they will not have the emotional checks and balances that their older colleagues have cultivated. They will share truths the senior folks won't.

Now, Listen Here…

I have read an awful lot of business books, especially as I prepared these thoughts for you. It struck me that no one ever tells you they screwed up. To underscore the infinite importance of listening, for the big stuff and the small, let me break with this tradition by telling you about one of my earliest presentations, which was for the French Government Tourist Board account. It was a huge and prestigious opportunity for our little agency, Ketchum Advertising. I was twenty-two years old. The main contact at the tourist board was an elegant man named George Hern. He was expansive and gregarious and everyone loved and admired him, especially the French government. He even got some very special citations from the highest places in France for his service, and he wore these proudly on his lapel. Soon into the process, George took me under his wing and became quite a mentor, and things were tracking along very well toward the final presentation.

On the day of the presentation, we were all assembled in the boardroom of our agency awaiting the arrival of the French delegation. The walls were adorned, everyone at the ready. A shrill ring of the conference phone on the wall pierced the quiet of anticipation. I went over, and picked it up.

"Hello?"

"Kevin, it's George."

"Hi George, yes, we're all ready and waiting to see you."

"Kevin, GOOD GOD, IT'S HERE!!!!"

I'd gotten the meeting place wrong. I stood frozen, while a jolt of electricity started from my head and coursed down to my feet and back. "Ah, I see," I said, not wanting to alarm my colleagues, and, more importantly, draw attention to my colossal screwup. Can you imagine, my first time out, having to tell the entire assembly of senior management that I got the meeting location wrong? My future hung in the balance. How would I explain myself? George continued, "Now Kevin, hang up and tell them there has been a mix-up. Say nothing more and just get here as quick as you can."

I hadn't listened, the most important skill in this game. I told my colleagues there had been a mix-up and we would need to race over to the client's offices right away. So, we hurriedly packed up and raced across town. We arrived, settled in, and George stood and opened the meeting. "Well, my friends, you all know that I am getting on in years and I am so terribly sorry for mixing up this meeting, and Kevin, many thanks to you and your team for being so gracious." He took the blame right then and there. This man, with whom I had created an emotional bond, was not only willing, but amusingly happy, to take the blame for it all. The reason: the existence of a bond of understanding. It was my first lesson that connecting with people on a deeper level means that, no matter what happens, whatever mistakes you might make, they will follow and support you.

George, wherever you are, I certainly didn't deserve what you did for me, but I sorely appreciated it (and still do). I learned a big lesson that listening is a pitchman's most important skill. (P.S.: We were awarded the business.)

And Now...

We have now concluded our investigation of the *who*. Next, let's connect with these people by digging deep for your special gifts, your *leverageable assets*, and making an irrevocable bond with your prospect, your audience, and your following.

REMEMBER THIS

. . . .

The search for the hidden agenda is the search for desire. It is rarely in evidence. You will need to put on special antennae to receive these signals. What is required is emotional insight, human sensitivity, thoughtfulness, empathy, and very good listening skills. Remember: *the brief is not the brief; be receptive; think like a shrink; listen in the right way; and ask the right questions.*

PART II

WHAT? CONNECTING TO THE HIDDEN AGENDA

4

Your Core

. . . .

Your *core* is your essence, the special abilities you possess at the core of your being. It is the special gift you have been given that separates you from others. The core is used to connect to the need, because it is something special you have that fulfills what your buyers lack. You are joined because they see you have the solution.

A Flight of Confidence

It was the year 2000. Fireworks displays were being tracked live on CNN in perfect sequence as midnight struck in each time zone across the globe. There was one place where the fireworks were perhaps particularly special, the fireworks over the Brandenburg Gate in Berlin.

At the turn of the millennium, I was at McCann in London, working with our ninety-plus European offices in their business development efforts. Our folks in Germany rang me with some very good news. They were on the short list for an account with Lufthansa German Airlines. We knew this could be not only a shot in the arm for our office there, but a fantastic global win to boot. Up to that point, I had spent a lot of time in Germany. I have quite an affinity for the country, and can trace my family origins to a small town in Bavaria. My ancestors on my mom's side, Great Grandmother Schneider and her eleven kids, came to the United States in 1882. I actually speak a bit of taxicab German as well.

In the run-up to the presentation, we began in earnest to meet with as many Lufthansa people as possible (remember the interview?). What was absolutely clear from these was the uniformly exuberant pride of the airline's employees. To their way of thinking, Lufthansa was, in every way, the best airline in the sky. Looking closely at every aspect of what the company did and how they did it, we saw those employees were right.

Meanwhile, we at McCann had set out to build a center of excellence of our own, with the first major agency network in Berlin, the restored capital city, now a source of enormous German pride. The agency would be unique, creating global communications across all platforms and customer touch points from one center of excellence to all parts of the McCann global system.

The fireworks over Berlin at the turn of the century marked a special moment in German history. The arrival of the new millennium was a turning of the page, heralding a new generation and a vibrant future for Germany. I can recall Berliners boasting to me as I once gazed over Berlin from atop the Brandenburg Gate, "There are more cranes in Berlin than anywhere in the world!" (The vast development in Dubai and Shanghai had not yet begun.) By the same token, many shared that there was a schism at work: the increasing confidence and German pride contrasted against the backdrop of the past. To me, the hidden agenda at Lufthansa was clear:

We want to assert that we are the very best in the air but are concerned it may be seen as aggressive or arrogant.

We at McCann learned there was a reticence at Lufthansa to make such a declaration given all the baggage of the past; now the millennium had come, however, Lufthansa was a superlative airline, and it should be encouraged to declare itself so. To connect with this hidden agenda was to state the facts, which were unequivocal. On a host of dimensions, Lufthansa was far and away an industry leader, setting standards in everything from route, to aircraft innovation, to maintenance and in-flight services. The answer: German pride is not taboo. In fact, two words described the airline perfectly: pride and excellence.

Connecting the Core

The key to winning Lufthansa was to connect to a core of excellence and pride shared between us. We decided we would not pitch to them out of our offices in Frankfurt, but instead share with them the dream we had, to be the first network agency to build a proud, new, contemporary presence in Berlin. Of course, this was practical and answered their brief—they wanted state-of-the-art global communications services—but in truth, what meant more was our shared vision for Berlin as a symbol of German confidence and pride. And what really captured them was what we would communicate.

On the day we opened the meeting, I told the Lufthansa executives that this meeting was about pride and excellence, theirs and ours. I spoke of our shared leadership, of McCann as the number-one agency in the world and now the number-one agency in Berlin. I then removed a cardboard screen on the table adjacent, and there sat a two-foot scale model of a Lufthansa "Super Constellation" aircraft, circa 1955. In a flash, one of the Lufthansa executives exclaimed, "It's a Super Connie!" I confirmed he was right. It was a much-beloved centerpiece of the Lufthansa fleet at the time and a symbol of Germany's move forward in the postwar era. It represented, and continues to represent, a heritage of excellence. I continued, "You have always been, you are, and you always will be the very best airline that flies. At this special moment, there is no better time for you to declare your category leadership." At that point, a fantastic creative director from our team, whose father was a Lufthansa pilot and whose mother was a Lufthansa flight attendant, presented a simple line, *"There's no better way to fly."* Smiles all around.

Connection to the hidden agenda that inspired the Lufthansa executives demonstrated our appreciation for their hidden agenda to talk to their rightful place of excellence in aviation, all driven by a shared core of pride and excellence. The business was awarded to us, and, I am proud to say, the concept and the relationship have continued for more than ten years.

The Truth That Lies Within

Finding the core means stripping all else away to reveal the brilliance that is purely you. This is ultimately what connects. I learned this from my inauspicious beginnings in advertising, which I started very much through the back door. As you'll later learn in some detail, I worked with Marriott International both during and after college in the foodservice arena.

This was hardly the kind of background that interested the glamorous folks on Madison Avenue (yes, they really were located on Madison Avenue...). I was turned away by virtually every major agency because of my lack of relevant experience. While thumbing through the pages of *Advertising Age* one day, I saw a profile on ad agencies in the food service business, those who did advertising for companies like Marriott. Eureka!

There was a little company called The Food Group, and I found the name of its CEO and founder—a fellow named Don Axelroad and proceeded to ring him every Monday for literally four months. His secretary, a lovely lady who never lost patience, answered the phone, "Oh, hello Mr. Allen, oh I'm very sorry, Mr. Axelroad isn't in at the moment. I will let him know you called." I could literally recite her response along with her. (I was tempted, but never did.) Finally I called at 8:30. I dialed and the phone was answered, only this time the husky voice said, "Don Axelroad..." I stuttered and stammered, "Er, this is Kevin Allen calling." A shocked Don replied, "Oh my God, it's you! What on earth do you want?!" I replied in an instant, having recovered myself, "I want a job!" He chuckled and referred me to his partner, a man by the name of Harry Delaney. But now, how to pitch Harry?

I rolled up at the appointed time and, after some small talk, Harry, a stereotypical "adman" and consummate salesman, asked me his first and virtually only question: "Well, you've got no marketing or advertising experience; why should I hire you?' I declared, "I am an enthusiastic and hard-working guy, people like me, and I am your target. I am a *food service insider.* I know more about your audience than you guys do!" Harry smirked, looked at me, and replied, "Okay, wise guy, let's see." He gave me a project. Find out everything I could about tomatoes (turns out he was pitching Del Monte). After two weeks and a successful recitation on the fascinating subject of the noble tomato (did you know tomatoes are a fruit?), Harry called me into his office with the following news, "Look, you have absolutely no experience. You've never worked in an agency, you have no marketing background, I don't know why I'm doing this—you got the job."

This was a wonderful start, and I learned tons from both Harry and Don. But what I really learned, on reflection, was to identify and apply my *core*. That is to say, I found a vital, relevant, and genuine part of my core experience and personality, and I matched it to a relevant context. I loved my tenure with this wonderful little company and was looked after like a wayward son by these generous people. Ambition called, and I soon found myself an account executive with a venerable Pittsburgh-based ad agency called Ketchum, MacLeod & Grove.

Out of a Nearby Phone Booth...It's Perfect Man!

I was now out of the womb and amongst the sharks. I soon came to the conclusion that if I was to compete effectively I would need to adopt a whole new stance: Kevin the Business Titan. In blue suit, white shirt, red tie, and wing-tip shoes, I adopted a demeanor that was a cross between that of Sean Connery and Walter Cronkite. I convinced myself that in order to succeed, I would need to conform to a set of standards of dress and demeanor that were aligned with a stereotypical corporate success story. My pitch was simple: I was perfect. To meet me was to form an impression that I had just walked off the polo field or had spent the afternoon in the library of the

University Club and was preparing to jet off to a distant capital to hobnob with other captains of industry.

One afternoon, I found myself addressing my colleagues in the agency in preparation for a new business pitch. There I was, holding forth to the group in my worldly manner, reciting the facts and figures of our prospect, when the door opened gently and a distinguished gentleman slipped in and made his way to the back of the room.

It was Bill Genge.

This impeccably dressed, elegant man with a shock of pure white hair, a former World War II fighter pilot, was the chairman of the agency. He was beloved, highly respected, extraordinarily dignified, and we all worshiped him. For me, the worshipping took place from afar, as I had never met him before. He just happened to be in town and was curious to see what the New York team was up to. I pressed on in my worldly demeanor. When we broke, Bill wandered up to me at the coffee station, put his arm around me, and said, "Son, that was one darned fine presentation. But can I give you a piece of advice? Why not step out from behind that blue suit and be yourself. It's what we all want to see and love about you.

I was absolutely stunned. How was it possible that this man, whom I'd never laid eyes on before, could see behind my worldly facade and knew that lurking behind it was a real person, the real Kevin, who he believed the world wanted to see?

I was laboring under the huge misconception that the slightly eccentric, exuberant, sensitive (yet perceptive), and somewhat goofy part of me was not in any way characteristic of someone who succeeded in business. Faced with this belief, I adopted the characteristics I associated with day-to-day business effectiveness and with that most important goal, climbing the ladder. It turns out I was not alone in this kind of thinking, as this had been very much part of corporate life since the 1950s. In fact, this viewpoint and behavior were actually codified by a guy named William Whyte in a book called *The Organization Man*. In certain rigid corporate cultures, the individual is effectively subsumed by the corporate entity. In order to be successful, members of the company are encouraged to essentially give themselves over to the company, sacrificing their individuality for the overall corporate good. Their personalities and individualities are surrendered for the sake of corporate "belongingness." Dreadful.

At the end of the day, your core is your passport to success. Success does not require abject psychological surrender to the organization you work with. Having initially believed that my own personality was no ticket to the desirable destination of corporate success, I learned that to be successful was to be myself. No easy task. Why? I think because there's a lot of "training," overt and otherwise, that suggests that there's a certain kind of characteristic that makes for successful people. The question is: How do you choose among all the facets of who you are to know what the core is?

Success in winning business and creating a following means coming across as your own genuine self and allowing others to see you as you are, all in the name of making a human connection. Bill's advice to me was right, because as Perfect Man I may have been talking, but I was certainly not connecting. Perfect Man is a hollow core, not a genuine person. The person (or team or company) your audience needs to see is a rich mosaic of characteristics that they will be drawn to and will bond with through affinity and even a little bit of curiosity. The search for your core is a quest to find and, perhaps more importantly, to believe in your true and compelling assets.

Any pitch to a person or an organization is only credible when it reflects an essential truth of what you're about. Finding this truth and having the courage to shine a light on one key element to the exclusion of others is a difficult process requiring discipline and self-confidence. Without this core, there is no clarity as to how you add value or what the compelling impetus is for people to follow you. *It comes from within you. Nowhere else.* It is the truth that lies within. This true 'voice" was captured in a wonderful poem:

I Am Not I

I am not I.
I am this one
walking beside me whom I do not see,
whom at times I manage to visit
and whom at other times I forget.
who remains calm and silent while I talk,
and forgives, gently, when I hate,
who walk where I am not,
who will remain standing when I die.
　　　　　—Juan Ramón Jiménez

I first heard this haunting poem, read aloud by poet Robert Bly, at a weekend retreat for the senior male members of McCann Erickson. The retreat was designed to break down the tough male stereotype at McCann, and the gathering was documented by a reporter from *Adweek*, Greg Farrell, who entitled his article "The Wild Men of McCann: What Happens When a Hard-Charging, Male-Dominated, Ego-Driven Agency Culture Is Asked to Get in Touch with Its Inner Self." The retreat itself was inspired by a remarkable and unforgettable man named Peter Kim, then McCann's vice-chairman, who saw it as part of the mountain-moving change he was implementing at the agency.

The weekend was presided over by Robert Bly. Tough, battle-hardened McCann veterans soon, when exposed to the magic of a storyteller and sage like Bly, stripped off their war faces. What was revealed was a quirky and altogether remarkable set of people, certainly not the one-dimensional warriors who had first set foot in the place. Hearing this poem, recited by Bly as he plucked the string of a haunting instrument called a *tar*, riveted all of us and, as we reflected on it, taught us that there is a true self that lies within, special and profound. I learned that the most important thing in any endeavor you undertake—at the core of your place in the world—is *you*... the real you. This is the "you" that people will follow. And for me, it was the man Bill Genge told me to be.

 ## Ok, Here's How...

Finding your core, and that of your organization (and that of your prospects, for that matter), is a mining operation. It requires digging deep to find a special central character that is genuinely yours. Finding your core is also an acknowledgment and acceptance process and then...it's a celebration of your special gifts. You'll note here, I speak of both you *and* your organization. *That's because, at the end of the day, you and your organization connect to people, not to a faceless entity. People are emotional creatures.* Here are three ways you can mine for your core:

1. Associative Method

Associative methods use words and images to evoke meanings that reflect your own true characteristics. Associating is a helpful technique because it uses recognized symbolism to sort through characteristics to find those that best describe you. Associative methods also provide a window on how others who have observed you and your organization in action see you. These are the people you know who know you well, warts and all. I call them your "board of directors." These are the members of your fan club. People who adore you, believe in you, and know you intimately. They can come from either your personal or professional life They're not your official board (perish the thought), but those people who know you and adore you unconditionally. They'll be frank about what you are and are not. When working with executives, I ask them to consult with those close to them, and have those people describe the executives' key strengths, characteristics, and abilities in a simple e-mail; then the executives follow up with a chat. The result is always illuminating, clarifying, and confidence building.

There are two excellent methods you can use to arrive at a description of your core:

Core Questionnaire

These are a few simple but probing questions that call upon you to be decisive about who and what you are. They are discriminatory by their nature, and ask that you choose among a sea of characteristics that stand out from all the others. It's not that you don't have other characteristics, you no doubt do, it's deciding which ones define you (or your organization).

I am unique because I _____.

People know me to be _____.

I am good at _____.

*I am different because I*_____.

What makes me special is my _____.

Core Word Sort

Sometimes answering these sorts of questions brings on writer's block: You sit staring at the page. The exercise below provides a bit of stimulus. Here, I draw on an excellent technique we used over the years when developing brands. From the pre-selected list of words, choose six that best describe your (or your organization's) core. It's actually a lot of fun and a great team-building exercise. Be careful when working in groups, though; finding your core is a decisive act, not a compromise or a consequence of consensus.

Smart	*Creative*	*Transparent*	*Diverse*
Irreverent	*Secure*	*Entrepreneurial*	*Goal oriented*
Elegant	*Pioneer*	*Risk Taker*	*Realist*
Challenger	*Activist*	*Explorer*	*Initiator*
Fixer	*Connector*	*Architect*	

One of my clients reached out to his board, some clients, and others close to him in his industry, and did the same exercise for his company. Here is what he got back:

Intelligent
Formidable
Wise
Influential

These characteristics inspired the basis of the company's expansion by invigorating the core of who they are and what makes them special. These characteristics were reflected faithfully in their go-to market platform and in the way they connected to clients and prospects. Management and employees recognized it and believed firmly in it. It is no accident that they are exceeding their growth plans handsomely.

2. Projective Methods

The MasterCard pitch was, when I look back on it, the most protracted and most difficult I have participated in. This was because of the nature of the product: a little piece of plastic with a logo on it. Therein lay the purity of the pitch: complete and utter product parity (there are no differences in form or function between Visa or MasterCard) with no extraneous issues, be they product features or other aspects of marketing advantage. The essence of what the MasterCard brand stood for needed to be found and leveraged. Day after day we struggled, with no results. We tried everything from analogies to myths, always ending up at the same dead end. All the while, we sweated, ever mindful that each passing day with no direction took us one step closer to pitch day, and we had nothing to show.

Our strategic team, at work on a dozen different tracks, decided to try a method to see what it might offer: a projective technique. The projective technique is a psychological profile test in which a variety of stimuli are used to evoke associations and underlying feelings and emotions. The most famous is the Rorschach, or inkblot, test, which takes otherwise abstract images and records people's feelings and associations after they are exposed to the images. For our projective test, our team devised a set of photographs, about fifty in all, showing everything from a shark to a baby. The collection was enormously varied, with the intention of provoking the widest range of feelings and ultimately helping consumers make a choice. In doing so, they'd give us some insight and direction. Groups of consumers were asked to choose from among these photographs the ten that best represented the core DNA of MasterCard and its nearest rivals, Visa and American Express. Then, they were asked to select one among the ten that they deemed to be the closest association with the brand.

On the day of the results, we all assembled to anxiously await our breakthrough, a hopeful, exciting representation that would give us direction and win us the pitch. The first photo, which the photo consumers had chosen as emblematic of AmEx, showed a well-dressed businessman boarding a Learjet. Then came the Visa image, attractive young urbanites at a ski lodge having drinks and socializing. Then came MasterCard's...drumroll...a picture of a little suburban house with the porch light on.

Our hearts sank. What on earth were we to do with such a dull association?

So, here we were, only weeks away from our presentation and no closer to a breakthrough, until our strategic group began to try to understand the associations of this little house and to figure out why it was selected. They discovered that the porch light evoked MasterCard because it was a brand that was involved in the everyday lives of ordinary people rather than catering to the highflying Learjet crowd or martini-swilling urbanites. MasterCard was seen as a more genuine, down-to-earth card that stood for the everyday. This was our core. But how could it be leveraged?

People, our team observed, had moved away from the ideals of the high-rolling '80s toward more authentic, substantive, inner-directed values. What was initially seen as boring and mundane, a simple little house, was actually an electrifying and powerful breakthrough. MasterCard was all about good, genuine people buying good things for good reasons. This, as you will see later, was the platform that led to the idea that changed everyone's lives, and now "Priceless" is in dozens of countries around the world, still running after more than a decade.

Here are two projective techniques you can use to get at the core:

Core Picture Sort

They say that a picture is worth a thousand words. It's true. Using imagery to assist you in looking at your core is not only fun but very effective. You tend to select a picture on instinct, then set out to derive meaning from it. This is why therapists use it to good effect! One way to do this on your own is to buy a random set of magazines. Pick a broad-based weekly, as well as magazines from a cross-section of areas, like fashion, lifestyle, and the like. Be sure the magazines are as diverse as possible. Then, leaf through the pages; when a picture appears that instinctively grabs you, tear it out. Your objective is to get ten that truly reflect who you are. Then earmark the three that are closest to your core, and then, ta-da! pick the one that most reflects you. Once you have done this, write down the words or characteristics represented in the picture you have chosen. These are the elements of your core.

Core Celebrity Sort

Another projective method uses widely recognized individuals. This is revealing because well-known people evoke for us certain core characteristics that we associate with them. For example, your collection of people might include:

Richard Branson	*John Lennon*	*Katharine Hepburn*
Robert De Niro	*Jonas Salk*	*John Kennedy*
Albert Einstein	*Lady Gaga*	*Harrison Ford*
Morgan Freeman	*John Wayne*	*Tom Hanks*
Gene Hackman	*Shirley MacLaine*	*Halle Berry*
George Patton		

Select the people who best represent your character, and are most like you. Let your instinct do the picking. Then, with your ten celebs selected, write down at least three words you associate with each individual you've picked. From this list, as you did in the word sort, select ten words, then three, then one.

3. The Footprint

The *Footprint* is a wonderful tool that combines a number of the elements we reviewed to form a profound imprint of the core of the company, brand, or person. It comes from one of my brilliant colleagues, Eric Einhorn, McCann Erickson's Chief Strategy Officer. Eric is a talented strategist and visionary and was a key part of the MasterCard team. He is a great thinker and distiller and his footprint defines the core of a brand, company, and yes, a person to its essence through the identification of words in answer to two key questions, the *means* and the *is*. It forces a choice of those words that best describe *three primary meanings*, that is, what associations it possesses, and then asks to assign *three dominant personality traits*. Fabulous.

Its strength is in providing both a broader spectrum of definition while not losing the all-important requirement for distillation and decision-making. Eric's work during Master-Card opened up the thinking to the power of MasterCard's unassuming yet profound profile. To realize its power was to first understand its essence. Here it is, as we presented it.

MasterCard Footprint

*...Means **Everyday***
*...Means **Ordinary life***
*...Means **The Generic Card***

*...Is **Unassuming***
*...Is **Unpretentious***
*...Is **Practical***

In addition, it was to be used as a prescriptive, for what things could be:

MasterCard Prescriptive Footprint

*...Means **Everything That Counts***
*...Means **Real Life***
*...Means **The Best Way to Pay***

*...Is **Purposeful***
*...Is **Genuine***
*...Is **Resourceful***

You can take your word sort exercises to another level with the superb exercise in the search for your core. Thanks Eric!

4. Profiling Method

I love you. Ich liebe dich. Je t'aime. All express exactly the same sentiment, but in a different language. Profiling provides a means of ensuring that you can calibrate your pitch in such a way that no matter who you're speaking to it will be understood and celebrated. This is not intended to change who you are or what you believe, but to ensure that your pitch is expressed in a manner that your audience can appreciate most. It's based on human sensitivity. A good illustration was our pitch to Marriott.

Whether I was sweating in the dish rooms of Marriott In-Flite's airline catering facility in Newark, New Jersey, or sweating at a hotel near Marriott's Bethesda headquarters on the night of our pitch rehearsal, I could simply not get rid of the butterflies. As with every pitch I think I've ever done, we'd pledged to rehearse and get a good night's sleep, but there we were in the evening going through our material, a long night ahead of us. Then a fellow with a beautiful little baby in his arms popped his head into the meeting room. He smiled brightly and said, "Welcome to Bethesda, I hope everything is going well for you." Joe Okon, a kindhearted and thoughtful man, was a key marketing executive from Marriott. He was actually checking in to see if we were okay. We were amazed. After exchanging pleasantries, he left us to our rehearsal, wishing us good luck for the morning. The moment he left us we all agreed on what a lovely gesture it was. At the end of our chat I can still hear Nina, our creative director shout, "Yeah, and he is soooooooo logo!"

Logo?

In those early days at McCann, Jim Heekin, the industry's greatest quarterback, put together a talented yet wildly diverse team. Unlike the homogeneity of the old McCann group, the incredible diversity of this team was what made it so compelling. Margie, my new business partner, had the idea to sensitize the team to one another's personalities; even more importantly, we had to be sure we were effectively understanding our prospects' personalities. (Remember, one never says no to Margie....) She accomplished this sensitization by organizing an extraordinary meeting led by a gregarious, larger-than-life man by the name of Stuart Sanders, founder of Sanders Consulting. He'd developed a simple system that cleverly labeled each of the personality typologies, categorizing each of these differing "types" using the familiar elements of a print ad, a reference useful for ad agency types: "headline," "body copy," "illustration," and, you guessed it... "logo."

Stuart presided over our unruly group and channeled our enthusiasm over discovering this wonderful new tool. We were like a bunch of schoolchildren as we tallied up our responses to reveal our various profiles. (For my own part, I was identified as a complete and off-the-charts "logo.") With this type of tool, we knew how to identify and match Marriott's core because we had a tool that allowed us to dig to find it.

After this introduction to the power of profiling, I engaged extensively over the years with a variety of profiling types. I discovered the work of David Keirsey, who described four "temperament types" ("artisans," "guardians," "idealists," and "rationals") in his book *Please Understand Me*. Of the many licensed personality profiling tools currently available, one of the most widely used is the Myers-Briggs Type Indicator, or MBTI, which draws on Carl Jung's psychological types to understand and assess personality. At my company, we use DISC, a fantastic profiling tool based on a behavioral model developed in the 1920s by Dr. William Moulton Marston.

For your company, constructing a profile means assessing your organization's fundamental strengths. At McCann Erickson, in assessing our profile we recognized our long-standing tradition of competitiveness (and combativeness). This was reframed as an unrelenting effectiveness culture, which could be harnessed for McCann and for its clients (and was the very element that we applied when pursuing MasterCard).

What's Your Profile?

As a consequence of the differing natures of how each of these types relates to other types, reacts to situations, consumes information, and makes decisions, it is easy to see how vitally important it is to carefully decide:

1. Which profile are you?
2. What is the profile of your organization?
3. Which profile is each of the individuals to whom your pitch is directed?
4. How will the different profiles affect the way you put your pitch forward?

Rudy Giuliani, former New York City mayor, observed, "One of a leader's responsibilities is to meet the needs of those he or she leads. The point is not to alter your message depending on the audience, but to present it so that it can be understood by every one you are addressing." Think of determining your target as deciding to eat at an Italian restaurant, but realizing that there are a variety of menu items at that restaurant.

A Simple Profiling Tool

I set out some time ago to develop a simple platform that had both a broad application outside of advertising and a firm grounding in Jungian thinking. Now, clearly, there is no precise science to these typologies, only their roots in the truths found in Jungian psychology and its implication for people's tendencies and preferences. I found it necessary, as I began to work with an array of companies, to adopt a broader terminology than those found in other profiling systems. But I think my choice of names for typologies really has to do with my inveterate love of Broadway: I use "script," "stage," "cast," and "marquee." It's fun, and we get to pick our favorite stars to describe folks we're pitching to. Here are my type descriptions:

Script People

These are process people, detailed, thorough, and orderly. They enjoy the process and methodology as much as (and maybe more than?) the result. People who cherish what they create, they are inner-directed and logical, and they value facts, clarity, and that which is familiar. Script people are engaged through an unemotional sequence of logic and proof. As the detectives say, "Just the facts, ma'am!"

Stage People

These people want action and directness. They expect you to listen, and everything is about getting things done. Stage people expect others to be precise and to the point. No beating around the bush for these folks. Confident and aloof, they value brevity, crispness, and a good debate. Challenging and decisive, they make decisions through unemotional analysis, after which quick action is required. Wagons, ho!

Cast People

These are "people" people. They view the world through the lens of human sensitivity and relationship. Consensus builders, they are sensitive and open, and they take others into account in everything they do. This empathy and value of friendship guides both their personal and their professional engagements. They are able to see all sides and they make decisions by virtue of their effects on people. Imaginative and kindhearted, cast people drive for harmony and consensus. How do you solve a problem like Maria?!

Marquee People

Expansive, energetic, and idea-driven, *marquee* people place a priority on creative thinking and possibilities. They are big-picture people and are all about adventure and inspiration. Highly verbal (give them a good listening to!), they relish stimuli and being in the limelight. They place a great deal of stock in the daring, new, and uncharted. "I know how to solve this problem; let's put on a show!!"

This process is applicable to organizations as a whole, not only to individual personalities. So it's a very good practice to profile the company, too. Lufthansa was decidedly a "script" client. As a consequence, we made sure to have mountains of material demonstrating our methodology, procedures, measurement practices, and other operational data that would efficiently create and distribute communications to their global infrastructure.

Wing-Tip Shoes

You may recall during my perfect man phase, a key ingredient was my wing-tip shoes.

I'm afraid to say they met an untimely end. It was a summer day in New York City. I was walking briskly from Penn Station to The Food Group's offices on Thirty-Fourth Street. I was wildly self-conscious about these shoes, as I always felt my feet were much too big (they're a size twelve). Honestly, the shoes felt like gunboats, like they were a block long. In spite of my feelings of self-consciousness, my ambition to be equipped with the right "captain of industry" clothing won out until I reached Second Avenue. On the corner was a fellow dressed in jeans and a hooded sweatshirt with a little table in front of him. He was selling socks, tube socks, to be precise, the long athletic ones with little red and blue stripes at the top. "Tube socks, get your tube socks here!" he exclaimed. "Two dollars apiece!" Just at that moment, he looked down at my enormous wing-tip shoes and said, "And you can get a pair for them big dogs, too!" The wing tips came off that evening and went in the closet.

They're still there.

And Now...

There are many people whose belief systems drive everything they do. They have an all-encompassing set of values and practices, which is the lens though which they see the world, relate to one another, and, above all, make decisions. It is the *credo*.

REMEMBER THIS

Your *core* is your essence, the special abilities you possess at the core of your being. It is the special gift you have been given that separates you from others. Any pitch for a person or an organization is only credible when it reflects an essential truth of your special and compelling assets. Your core is how you add value, and it provides a compelling impetus for people to follow you. It comes from within you, nowhere else.

5

The Credo

. . . .

Credo means literally "I believe." Any pitch has, as a key element, the abiding and sincere beliefs of the individual or company making that pitch. The credo connects to the values, because it is a belief system you and your audience share. You are joined because you best understand the company's fundamental beliefs and guiding principles.

The Mystery Visitor

Desperate to make money for my college tuition, I landed a job at Marriott In-Flite Services (the airline-catering division of Marriott International). I began at JFK airport, New York, forty-five minutes from my house. I couldn't believe my good fortune. For the first month I mopped floors. Then one day, out of the blue, I was taken around to the loading dock. There sat a shiny new apple red Ford Country Squire station wagon. "Here's your car," my foreman said. "You'll be working on the field." I was utterly thrilled with the idea of cruising around the airfield amid the hustle and bustle of flight movements. He then told me what I would actually be doing. He showed me to the rear of the car and opened the doors. There they were, six huge cases of toilet paper. "Your job is to stock each of the toilets on the aircraft. A 747 gets seventeen rolls, a DC-8 63 gets eleven. Get going."

There is a very distinct hierarchy at the airport, with the flight mechanics at the top of the pyramid and others arrayed beneath them. Needless to say, I held a post lower than the low, and as my bright red car stocked with toilet paper arrived at every aircraft the guys would call out, "Hey, here comes the TP man." So much for my big promotion.

I continued to work at Marriott during summers and weekends until I graduated from college. Not knowing what I was going to do after graduation, I accepted a position as shift manager at one of Marriott's largest airline catering facilities. I had gone from TP man to a shiny new position as assistant manager at the Marriott in-flight catering unit, building number 139 at John F. Kennedy International Airport. I presided over the night shift, and occupied a little dispatch office on the second floor. For security, it had an intercom system to the front door and a crooked little truck mirror we affixed to the wall that gave a poor but adequate view of the entrance door. I rotated my shift with a very nice, highly energetic guy, who, among other things, was a constant prankster. One evening he regaled me with one of his many stories.

It seems that while he was alone on his shift in the little dispatch office, at around 11:15 p.m., the quiet of the evening was pierced by the ringing of the security doorbell. He pressed the intercom and asked, "Who is it?" A few men in trench coats were barely visible in the street below. Crackling through the intercom, a voice came back, "It's Mr. Marriott."

Thinking this a ploy to enter the premises for a shakedown, he thought for a second and replied, "Oh yeah, well I'm Dick Tracy…take a hike!" Some days later, I heard that Mr. Marriott was in the area. He was well known for his surprise visits. I immediately thought, Holy moly! Did he really turn Mr. Marriott away? Did Mr. Marriott really turn up? Was that really him? Did he really tell him to take a hike? We'll never know…

I later learned that J.W. "Bill" Marriott Jr. had in fact visited the facility. I was keenly interested in learning about his visit and what he said. From what I could glean, he spoke simply, without notes, and in a friendly, conversational manner. He told the employees present that they were part of an extended family and that everyone had a special and important role to play, however small, in serving our customers. He spoke of a core belief that began with his dad, J. Willard Marriott. He believed that Marriott's first priority was the good treatment of its employees, that, "If you take care of your employees they will take care of the customer." For my part, working a night shift when this wonderful man spoke to my colleagues was sorely disappointing, but I did get a consolation prize, a book called *Marriott*, written by J. Willard Marriott, the founder of the company. In the quiet of my little dispatch office I pored over the pages of down-home wisdom and the simple yet profound values of this remarkable man who built a remarkable company. He spoke of things I had learned as a kid from my wonderful mother, of the importance of hard work, of human kindness and generosity. It thrilled me that these values were not only precious, but were a recipe for success in business. In the loneliness of that little office I felt that I had a big role to play and perhaps the person I was, with the beliefs I held, really could be a recipe for success. Like his father before him, J.W. "Bill" Marriott believed that to be in service was a noble and honorable calling. No matter what task we were performing, none were considered menial, because each job had a role to play in creating a happy and pleasant experience for the customer. In his own thoughtful manner, Bill Marriott shared a key part of his and Marriott's credo.

McCann's Big Break

Fifteen years later I had reached one of the greatest achievements of my life: I'd made the long slog from tiny little agencies to a position as account director with the biggest agency in the world, McCann Erickson Worldwide. This great titan had stumbled with the loss of Coca-Cola in the early 1990s. I found myself part of a new team struggling to turn around this giant dreadnought. Instinctively, we knew the answer was the pursuit of new and different kinds of accounts. We knew the promise of what McCann could become would be our way out. One Monday morning, as I was flipping through the pages of Adweek a headline leaped out at me: "Marriott shops for agencies." I couldn't believe what I was reading. Could it be possible that the company where I got my start would become the account that staged the turnaround for McCann?

The Letter

The first step in pitching to Marriott was the solicitation: I had to break through the doorway. Getting through to any marketing director is a near-impossible task, so I started with his secretary. Rather than write three pages about all the marvelous things that McCann Erickson had done, I decided my pitch would be based on Marriott and McCann's shared beliefs. I went back to those quiet nights in my little dispatch office and the words from *Marriott* that inspired me so.

I wrote a simple one-page letter introducing myself as a former Marriott employee now working for McCann. I asserted that we were a lot like Marriott, and I reminded her of something J. Willard Marriott often said, "I get a lot of letters from our customers, they don't tell us how wonderful our ballroom was, they tell us how wonderful our people are. If you're interested in your job, you can do anything." And perhaps at the core of his beliefs was this sentiment: "We started this business to render a good service to people, for a good purpose." I told her how compatible we would be as client and agency because the wonderful people we assembled at McCann lived according to the same credo.

I called a few days later and reached an effervescent lady who said, "Yes, I got your letter, you quoted Mr. Marriott Sr!" We chatted pleasantly and she made it clear that the letter would go directly to the top of the pile for the director of marketing. A few days later we were in. In point of fact, the letter was accurate. We at McCann were an eclectic group of loonies: We all came together sharing a collective *real ambition* for the renaissance of McCann, united in our belief that our emphasis should be not on the "empire" but on creating a great experience for our clients.

Our Key to Victory

We were briefed by the prospective client, which was a very pleasant process, befitting the culture of Marriott. A good deal of time was spent on the changing dynamics of the hotel category. It seemed that the business was becoming over developed, and Marriott's position was challenged from a variety of quarters, notably folks like Hyatt, with their snazzy atriums, and Westin, with their up-market cachet. Marriott must keep evolving, it was declared, and needed to be seen as contemporary, and as appealing as these newcomers. I could see in the process, though, an internal dilemma that arose from embracing new developments: How could Marriott deal with the "sexier" tone and appeal of its new rivals, yet still be true to what the Marriott brand was all about? *The hidden agenda:*

> *We value the importance of being at the cutting edge of the lodging industry, but do not want to compromise our values in the process.*

Given our sense of the importance Marriott placed on employees, it seemed only natural to begin there. We asked our youngest and brightest strategist to embark on a journey across the Marriott hotel empire to speak one-on-one with a range of Marriott people employed in all facets of their hotel business. The analysis translated into what we called "The Anatomy of a Hotel Stay." It was fascinating stuff (for example, one huge stress moment in any traveler's journey comes during the minutes she checks in—for a few moments, guests feel "homeless," until the person behind the counter confirms the reservation). But the thing that stood out most was the consistency of the attitude and genuine cheerfulness and kindness of Marriott's people. It was clear that they were actively concerned with the quality of their guests' stay. For me, this was no accident.

Someone remarked in the interviews that a fancy lobby made no difference if you were treated poorly. It was clear that, at the end of the day, it was how people felt and were served that mattered most. All of this exhaustive analysis, and a thorough immersion in the values of Marriott, helped distill all of our thinking into the essence of the Marriott International brand:

We believe that whatever the trend, whatever evolution we make, our cornerstone is a culture based on the honor and nobility of service.

This *credo*, central to their pitch and ours, was summarized in a simple sentence that represented everything the Marriott brand stood for, and to our delight and no small amount of surprise, it came from none other than the young fellow, John Kottman, who had crisscrossed the country in search of Marriott's real essence. This statement represented a code of ethics, behavior, and belief that all of Marriott's ambitions would be guided by. It was a promise to their employees and their customers.

"The Spirit To Serve": This sentiment, coined by our young strategist, and the resulting presentation captivated our Marriott audience. A few days later, fifteen years after I mopped my first floor in a Marriott flight kitchen, McCann Erickson was awarded the Marriott International business. *We won the*

Marriott business because we formed a shared bond, which both they and we at McCann believed, based on the idea that Marriott's most precious asset was not bricks and buildings but its people and their attitudes. We asserted that McCann, like Marriott, was made up of people, who, like our strategist John, were kind at heart and maniacal in their dedication; in our minds, that made for the greatest of partners.

Some years later it was J. W. "Bill" Marriott's turn to launch his own book, following in his father's footsteps. His achievements in taking a few hotel properties and building one of the most successful and exciting hotel networks in the world were chronicled in a description that highlighted what was really important to Marriott and indeed how these achievements were possible. In his book, he recounted the credo of Marriott, laying out the value systems he believed made for a great company.

I thought I would faint dead away when I first laid eyes on the title: *The Spirit To Serve: The Marriott Way.*

The Ties That Bind

Taken from Latin, *credo* means, literally, "I believe." A credo is the underpinning of an organization's culture and code of behaviors. It determines who joins, how they are led, and how the organization comports itself. Now, more than ever, a brand or company is judged not by what is says, or even what it sells, but by what it *believes*. Its actions are a direct reflection of its credo. As the role of communities grows, the vital element that will bind groups is their credo. Tribal in nature, the credo is a glue that holds communities together; the means through which you connect with these groups will not be any doorway other than the value system they hold dear. Ignite, share, and link genuinely to these values, and the people who hold them will follow you. Any pitch has, as a core element, the abiding and sincere beliefs of the individual or company making that pitch. People will follow you in large measure because they believe in you and what you represent. Crystallizing a belief system to create a following requires an ability to make clear what you value and to forge a shared bond between you and your audience. Your pitch's effectiveness in creating a following depends on the presence and clarity of your credo.

Rudy Giuliani's value system was a cornerstone of his mayoral race and of the successful turnaround of New York City. Among Rudy's most fundamental beliefs is *"You have to have them."* No organization can do anything without an understanding of what you, as a group, believe in and value. As Rudy and his team evidenced, belief can move mountains. I remember many statements of belief during his administration:

People created the problem, people can fix the problem.
What doesn't get measured doesn't get done.
It can be done and it will be done.

Key to the city's renaissance was a belief that the city represented an ideal, a great "city on a hill" that attracted people seeking a better life. The administration promoted New York as a place of rich diversity, where no one is better than another, all have an equal chance to make their mark, and no one is more special than another. Rudy was tough on special interests and evenhanded in applying the law. Everyone would be protected equally. Simple as that.

Credo, Etched in Stone

One of my all-time favorite examples of credo can be found embedded in the culture and literally in the halls of Johnson & Johnson, where a portion of the company's belief statement is etched in a slab of stone in their New Brunswick, New Jersey, headquarters:

We believe our first responsibility is to the doctors, nurses and patients, to mothers and fathers and all others who use our products and services. In meeting their needs everything we do must be of high quality.

We must constantly strive to reduce our costs in order to maintain reasonable prices.

Customers' orders must be serviced promptly and accurately. Our suppliers and distributors must have an opportunity to make a fair profit.

We are responsible to our employees, the men and women who work with us throughout the world. Everyone must be considered as an individual. We must respect their dignity and recognize their merit. They must have a sense of security in their jobs.

Compensation must be fair and adequate, and working conditions clean, orderly and safe. We must be mindful of ways to help our employees fulfill their family responsibilities.

Employees must feel free to make suggestions and complaints. There must be equal opportunity for employment, development and advancement for those qualified.

We must provide competent management, and their actions must be just and ethical.

We are responsible to the communities in which we live and work and to the world community as well. We must be good citizens—support good works and charities and bear our fair share of taxes. We must encourage civic improvements and better health and education.

We must maintain in good order the property we are privileged to use, protecting the environment and natural resources.

Our final responsibility is to our stockholders. Business must make a sound profit. We must experiment with new ideas. Research must be carried on, innovative programs developed and mistakes paid for.

New equipment must be purchased, new facilities provided and new products launched. Reserves must be created to provide for adverse times. When we operate according to these principles, the stockholders should realize a fair return.

These words, written originally by the company's founder, are no empty platitudes. These vital value systems, which embody humanity and fairness, are a distinct and clear description of the ethics the company has embraced for more than a hundred years. These values came into play when the McCann team competed for a new Johnson & Johnson account.

Relief from Johnson & Johnson

A division of Johnson & Johnson had been in development of a breakthrough product. It was designed for people suffering serious chronic pain from things like migraines and serious back injuries. For many who suffered terribly with debilitating pain, the product offered a miracle. The McCann team received a brief, which was quite straightforward, and we reviewed it with no real clue about how to proceed until someone on the team noticed that the preponderance of Johnson & Johnson people coming to see us, the ones who would be making the decision, were doctors. While these doctors were clearly responsible for marketing the product, we figured that they had more than a marketing stake in the success of this medication. Doctors take a Hippocratic Oath, and while they may be employed in marketing, their life's work is to make people well. This product represented a breakthrough that would provide relief to people who thought they could never have it. *The hidden agenda:*

We value the oath we took. This is not merely a marketing endeavor, but a journey toward making a difference in the lives of people who think there is no relief in sight.

This hidden agenda hugely influenced our pitch team and, by definition, what our pitch would be. To work on the pitch, we chose a group of individuals whose communications careers were rooted in the pharmaceutical category. More importantly, we identified several who had personal experience of chronic pain or whose loved ones suffered from this medical issue. One of our teammates was a chronic migraine sufferer, and shared with us the very difficult life of a person with this affliction, who often feels alone in the struggle because non-sufferers understand so little about how challenging it can be to function with chronic pain.

This story inspired us to organize a series of in-depth, one-on-one interviews with people in this community of chronic pain sufferers. These individuals were from all across the country and across all categories of chronic pain; all spoke about the lives they led coping with ever-present pain. It was simply heart-wrenching. The interviews galvanized our team, and we realized that the experience of chronic pain sufferers would form a core part of our strategic recommendation. Later we realized it would form the core part of our entire pitch.

On the day of the pitch, the clients filed into the conference room. On six easels were six blown-up photographs taken of individuals we had met. The opening speaker took the floor and said, "Before we introduce ourselves, and in the spirit of what we think our mission is here today, I would like first to introduce the six individuals you see here in the room. The first is Maria Gonzalez. She is a migraine sufferer. Her migraines are so severe that once a month she must lock herself in a room in the darkness to avoid pain. Her children do not understand and think, during this time, she doesn't love them." (This was taken directly from one of our interviews.) This passionate speaker then moved around the room, introducing the other five individuals, all chronic pain sufferers we had spoken with, and concluding with a simple statement, "What's important about this presentation, and more importantly about working with you, is that this is not merely a marketing endeavor, this is about working together to make these people well." We won, and when later asked why, they said, "Because you got it."

The Tribes of Our Age

Emotional and spiritual bonds tied to a belief system have been unifying communities throughout the ages. Early tribes developed a value system for what they held close and codified these values in an oral tradition. In some parts of the world these values are still enshrined in songs and poems handed down generation after generation. Families expressed their credos in coats of arms, each element a unique representation of a particular belief or value. Later, communities defined by physical boundaries, which evolved as nation states, would create flags bearing the symbols and credos of their communities.

Today, tribes are still with us but in bigger and more profound ways than ever before. Now, they are borderless communities fueled by digital technologies and platforms, and exist irrespective of national boundary. They are groups of individuals, very much like the tribes of old, held together by shared value systems or a common credo. This is what makes the world go 'round and its importance is greater than ever before.

So, central to an effective pitch is your ability to do what has been done through the ages, to codify, crystallize, and articulate your core beliefs into a credo for your community. A simple, compelling statement is a great way to do it.

  ## Okay, Here's How…

So, let's write a credo. We'll follow an exercise similar to the one we used when we chose our core. This time, though, our result will have greater emotional content than the more functionally driven core:

1. Associative Method

The methods for deriving the credo are similar in structure to those I shared regarding the search for your core. Used in countless brand marketing situations, each exercise is designed to help you to isolate your credo.

Credo Questionnaire

The first step is to reach in and do a bit of soul searching. Be sure you answer from the heart and give the first thought that comes to your mind, however it may sound to you. It must be something you feel strongly about, and have for some time.

What's important to me about the way I live my life?
What's important to me about how I work (and who I work for)?

Once you have arrived at your responses, set them aside for a day or two. Look at them again later and ask yourself the following questions about what you arrived at.

Why did I choose those particular values and what does each one mean to me in practical terms?
How do they guide my behavior?
If I was to start a new business, would I build it around this value?
Would I want to continue to stand for this value in a hundred years, even if the world changed around me?
Would I still hold this value even if it lost me money?
Do I believe that I wouldn't want to work with those who don't share this core value?

Credo Word Sort

Similar to the word sort exercise we looked at when determining your core, this exercise features a long list of values. As before, select ten that you believe are closest to your beliefs, then narrow to three, then select one. Following are a few examples.

optimistic	*relentless*	*patient*	*selfless*
demanding	*exacting*	*compassionate*	*curious*
trustworthy	*driven*	*persistent*	*eccentric*
honest	*pure*	*driven*	*elegant*
wise			

Do you remember your "board of directors"? Ask them to name the values they think you embody. Importantly, *ask them to tell you how you have lived these values each and every day.* Suggest that they list your values and how you have demonstrated and lived out the values they chose for you. You'll be amazed at what you get. Gather all the responses and write them down, each value on a single card. Then, prioritize those that you feel are at the core of what you believe. Here are mine:

Generosity of spirit
Optimism
Persistence

2. Projective Methods

As you did when finding your core, you can use the picture or celebrity sort to identify your credo, only this time you'll concentrate on values rather than traits. For variety, I'm offering another method, which I call the *logo sort*. Logos are powerful symbols, "vessels" that contain rich meanings. Looking through the list of logos, pick ten that symbolize a value system that is close to yours. Do the same exercise as before, narrowing to ten, then three, then one. Once you have done this, write down the values associated with the logo you've chosen. They will form the basis for your value system set, or credo.

Here are some sample companies with very well-known logos:

Disney	*Tiffany*	*Amnesty International*
American Express	*Harley-Davidson*	*Playboy*
MTV	*MasterCard*	*Microsoft*
Apple	*Mercedes-Benz*	*Nike*
Rolls-Royce	*The Red Cross*	*Greenpeace*
Johnson & Johnson		

Writing Your Credo

Letting Johnson & Johnson's stone credo inspire you (no, you don't need to have a slab in your front hall), write your own credo as a simple yet expressive bit of prose that ties together a united point of view. Begin the statement with these words: "I believe..." or "We (or your company's name) believe..."

The Family Credo

When I was eleven years old, my grandfather came to live with us. He was, and is to this day, my greatest hero. What I didn't know at the time was that this jovial, quirky man had about a year to live, having been diagnosed with throat cancer. A little room was built for him and crammed with his artifacts: dark wooden furniture, a great big armchair, and wall-to-wall books. Bill Whalen, my mother's dad, was a real estate broker but had not always planned to be one. At seventeen, he was painting utility poles in Springfield, Massachusetts, and one afternoon began his paint job by hanging his pot on a wire that some bozo had failed to turn off. He was shocked, thrown to the ground, and very badly burned. He recovered, miraculously, but was left with the use of only one hand and with an ungainly limp. When we kids asked him repeatedly why he limped, to our giggles, he would reply, "Oh, I'm just lopsided."

Every evening we would sit together in the armchair watching *The Untouchables* or perusing the many books he possessed, but we always came back to our favorite: *One Hundred and One Famous Poems.* To my delight, my grandfather would amuse me with "The Gingham Dog and the Calico Cat" or terrify me with "The Highwayman," but he always returned to our favorite, the one he called our battle cry:

INVICTUS

Out of the night that covers me,
Black as the pit from pole to pole,
I thank whatever gods may be
For my unconquerable soul.

In the fell clutch of circumstance
I have not winced nor cried aloud.
Under the bludgeoning of chance
My head is bloody, but unbowed.

Beyond this place of wrath and tears
Looms but the Horror of the shade,
And yet the menace of the years
Finds and shall find me unafraid.

122

The Credo

It matters not how strait the gate,
How charged with punishments the scroll,
I am the master of my fate:
I am the captain of my soul.
                         —*William Ernest Henley*

My grandfather taught me early that your beliefs and reputation were your most important possessions. He asserted, "Kevin, if you believe in something enough, you can make it happen, but in doing so you will get knocked down...and often." But, he offered, "This isn't the test of your strengths. The test is the fact that you *keep getting up*." Through the trying times of my youth and when battering down doors to build a career in the advertising business, his words have guided me, and they do so to this very day. *There is probably no step more important, or that will prove more resonant, or that will be more of a bond in the motivation and credibility of your pitch, than creating your credo.*

So sayeth the TP man.

And Now...

Connecting to your audience's hidden agenda means creating a bond. There are hidden agendas that suggest you connect by your core, what you both *are* and what makes your connection unique. There are also bonds based upon the credo, or what you both *believe*. There is another, the *real ambition* that you both share.

REMEMBER THIS

· · · · · · · · · · · · · · · ·

Your *credo* is central to your pitch. Any pitch has, as an essential element, the abiding and sincere beliefs of the individual or company making that pitch. People will follow you in large measure because they believe in you and what you represent. Crystallizing a belief system to create your following requires an ability to make clear what you value and to forge a shared bond between you and your audience. Your pitch's effectiveness in creating a following depends on the presence and clarity of a compelling credo.

6

Real Ambition

. . . .

Real ambition is the human desire to create something good where nothing existed before. It is a measure of your worth, and of the worth of your organization. It's a key element of what makes people follow you. The real ambition is used to connect to the want, because it is a vision shared by you and your clients of what the future will become. You are joined because your clients see that their ambitions are possible with you.

The Growth Aspirant

I am a Babylonian. Babylon on Long Island, New York, that is, a small town fifty miles from Manhattan. Every Sunday, my family piled into a 1953 Buick 88 (a black beast with no reverse) and did what everyone else did on that day—we visited grandparents for Sunday dinner. My family would inevitably arrive first, and sometime thereafter a loud bang at the door would be heard as the first of the Brooklyn contingent appeared with a shock of frighteningly frizzy hair, a smear of red lipstick, and a howl of "Hellooooooo." Aunt Francis (Franny, as she was also known) would burst through the door, trip on the ledge, and plummet to the foyer floor. As the entire family rushed to her aid she would say, on cue, "Oh, geez, I'm a bundle of noives!" It happened every Sunday, for as long as I can remember; I could go on about the other antics that ensued every Sunday, but let's just say Franny's entrance gives you a general idea of the tenor of our family get-togethers.

While all this was happening, I was inevitably glued to a stool in front of a little metal table where stood my grandfather's pride and joy, a Zenith Trans-Oceanic radio. It had been a Christmas present, purchased for him by my grandmother in 1938. With Bakelite headphones on my nine-year-old head, I would carefully turn the dial to pick up broadcasts from around the world in languages I'd never heard of, let alone understood. For hours I was transported to these faraway, enchanting places. One Sunday, I turned the dial in my usual manner, only this time heard "This is BBC World Service and now, Brahms' Piano Concerto no. 1 in D Minor." I was electrified. Who were these people? Where were they? They spoke so beautifully, they didn't shout, they didn't say "fougetaboudit." And how was it possible anyone could listen to such nice music? It was at this moment that I became a card-carrying member of the tribe of "growth aspirants."

It was clear to me, at the age of nine, that one day I would somehow leave Babylon and make my mark in the world of *BBC World Service* people, with accent to match. I later discovered that the *BBC* was not a place itself but was actually located in a city called London. Well, just a few years later, I found myself living and working in the city of BBC broadcasts and living out my *real ambition.*

Real Ambition: The Fuel of Your Pursuit

Ambition is strong desire, for good or bad. Alexander the Great had his ambition, but so did Michelangelo. Two different ambitions, two different results: to conquer or to create. I wonder whose fruits have endured? Ambition is a word that implies some sort of forward direction and sense of desired achievement. *Real ambition* carries with it a certain sense of what is right, it's an ambition that is for the collective good and that benefits all those who are involved or are touched by its movement. *Real ambition is the human desire to create something good where nothing existed before. It is a measure of your worth, and that of your organization. It's a key element of what makes people follow you.*

Would it be better if I called these dreams? Not for me. A dream is some sort of apparition. They're thoughts you go to in your sleep or when you drift off in geometry class. Real ambition is your own fiery desire to grow, to go from one state to an expanded one. Real ambition calls for you to be broader, fuller, more challenged, more stretched, and, I believe, more personally and professionally fulfilled. Dreams are thoughts… *real ambition is action.* It's clear, focused, identifiable—and honorable. Real ambition is the engine of your endeavor. It is a never-ceasing quest that drives growth aspirants toward a special "place." Pursuit of real ambition provides all-important direction for any pitch. It's one where the goal seems impossible but, through your connection with the hidden agenda, you rally people to believe it is within reach. Real ambition was certainly in evidence as Rudy Giuliani's quest for the mayor's office and for a safer city unfolded.

127

People Can Fix the Problem

Rudy's vision for the city of New York rested not only on what New York represented, but on what it had to become: *Safe, so that people could achieve their ambitions for themselves and their families.* Rudy's *real ambition* was to confront the impossible. He had to address not just the staggering crime rate but also the culturally embedded belief that nothing could be done about it. Rudy and his team members saw that the key to transforming New York City into a dramatically safer, more prosperous, more livable place began with an assumption: *"People created the problem, so people can solve the problem."* This took the "impossible" task ahead and expressed it in simple human terms that framed the entire task in a much more manageable way. It gave confidence that the task could be understood and a way forward developed.

The complexity of New York's turnaround cannot be overstated, but it was rooted in a simple real ambition. Every single strategy, every plan, and every element led back to this objective, to making the city safe so that seekers could realize their dreams. Every employee, every commissioner, and every police officer believed that they were acting in concert with the real ambition laid out by Mayor Rudy Giuliani.

In all my years as a pitchman, I had one pursuit in particular that holds a special place in my heart. It's the very finest example of what a real ambition can accomplish. It involved some very special people at a very special time.

HerdBuoys and South African Airways

Advertising is one of those industries that, by definition, will put you at the spearpoint of your client's desires. Your job: to distill the essence of your client's real ambition down to a mere thirty-second sound bite or a six-word headline. It is the crystallization of the company's pitch. As a former "mad man" of McCann Erickson Worldwide, I've had the great thrill and pleasure of participating in several very special pitches, developed and presented to the people of South African Airways by McCann Erickson's agency in South Africa.

At this time in my tenure with McCann, I was based in Europe. A call came in from Dimape Serenyane, a key guy in the newly reconstituted office of McCann Erickson in South Africa. An extraordinary man, Dimape grew up in Soweto and was responsible for the first election registration program ever attempted in the townships, a project he carried out at great risk. Dimape, along with two extraordinary men, Peter Vundla and Happy Ntshingila, formed an agency in the township, the first black agency in South Africa. They borrowed the name *Herd* from a customary vocation of young black South Africans, and co-opted *Buoy* from a term used by whites for black Africans. Happy recalls, "Peter, Dimape, and I called ourselves the Herdbuoys (with a tip of the cap toward a healthy, buoyant future in South Africa), not just because of the guiding role that this icon represented, but also because it is a symbol of great humility, a characteristic that would prove very important to the whole country in the future." HerdBuoys was born of a *real ambition* for the black people of South Africa to lead major business organizations in their country and, in Peter, Dimape, and Happy's case, to create an organization that played a role in providing role models for their emerging nation. Said Peter Vundla, "HerdBuoys was first not an ad agency, it was a movement! We were tired of white creatives in established agencies depicting Blacks in secondary or subservient roles: the maid; the gardener; the petrol attendant and sometimes the buffoon. We felt that the time had come to define ourselves as a people and reflect Blacks as how they could be in a normal society. So Blacks were always presented in aspirational terms in our ads."

Surprising New Leadership

Peter, Happy, and Dimape grew their agency rapidly, with breakthrough victories with South African Breweries, Unilever, and a stream of other significant new business wins. They were showing the country that brilliant black talent could out-pitch and out-advertise their competition, come what may. Seeing this momentum, McCann Worldwide approached them concerning their office in Johannesburg, an old-fashioned agency housed in colonial-style offices, strangely reflective of their position in the market. In an unprecedented move, the agency with its roots in the townships pulled a reverse takeover, with a substantial equity stake and management control of the McCann Erickson office there. One can only imagine the looks on faces, as the *HerdBuoys* walked into their offices taking over management of McCann.

Priceless!

The Agency was dubbed *HerdBuoys McCann*, reflecting a new direction for the company and indeed the country. I visited the agency in Johannesburg when it opened and saw firsthand the extraordinary cultural task ahead. The all-white agency, formerly housed in a staid British colonial building, was now an unprecedented experiment, ensconced in a wonderful building outside the traditional district with bright colors, inspired artwork, and sayings of the new South Africa adorning the walls. There was fallout, in clients and personnel, but a core group of aspirants remained, especially an inspired group across all racial lines.

Then it came. South African Airways, South Africa's national airline, announced an agency review, and we were one of four agencies invited to pitch for the business. Dimape asked if I could come down and look their recommendation over and, in particular, help coach their presentation. I flew out from London on a Friday and met with the team on Saturday morning. Led by Happy, with his irrepressible optimism and good humor, the team included an impressive young woman by the name of Sizakele Zwane and a creative director named John Smeddle. They had already been hard at work for many weeks, and they proceeded to present a thorough and detailed advertising recommendation. It was right. It was solid. But it needed something compelling to crystallize the agency's shared real ambition with its South African Airways prospect. I simply didn't know how to tell them other than coming out directly, "Guys, this is all very correct and disciplined, but it needs heart. You need to move them emotionally around your ambitions for them."

Taking the floor, Dimape and Happy spoke to the group, putting the airline's meaning in a context; they talked of their years in the townships, of organizing election registration, and of what the country was trying to become. They moved the group profoundly. I asked Sizakele, "What does South African Airways mean to you?" In a reflexive instant she replied, "All of our hopes." I replied, "Then this is what you *must* present!"

131

I asked them to place all of the work they had done to the side and to develop a summary piece on what South African Airways meant to them and to the country. The hidden agenda:

We want to be sure we do the right thing, because the eyes of the world are upon us.

We would meet again on Sunday, just twenty-four hours before the presentation. We returned to the conference room late Sunday evening, with nervous looks among the group as Sizakele and her colleague John took the floor: "We're going to do what every family does when they are proud of their loved ones; we're going to show you a photo album. This album is a family treasure, pictures of the family that comprises the new South Africa, the South Africa of all of our hopes." The team was mesmerized by this opening, and they continued by indicating that a series of photographs would be shown on a screen in a soft, rolling sequence, over which a lullaby would play. Not just any lullaby, but a beautiful song by the name of "Thula Mtwana," a lullaby that has been sung by both white and black South Africans for generations. It begins with a simple line, "Sometimes we feel blessed." As the beautiful tones of this enchanting song flowed, the mosaic of South Africa— beautiful faces, old and young, black and white—appeared and dissolved into one another with a mesmerizing cadence. All of this was summarized by a simple line at the close, *"We're South African."* I was absolutely floored. There, in living, moving color and melodic tones, was their *real ambition*, and it was a real ambition not just for an airline, but for their nation and their future.

On pitch day, the team assembled in front of stony-faced

airline executives and members of the central government. Dimape opened with his talk about the South Africa of his early life and its struggles. With not a pin drop to be heard, he turned the meeting over to his teammates, whom he described as the future of the country. After a thorough recitation of the recommendation, John turned on the video and played the film he and Sizakele had shared with me just a few hours before. The room was entranced, and every one of the executives was profoundly moved. I knew it was won then and there. I later learned the decision was unanimous, and many indeed *did* decide right then and there.

This was more than pitch idea or an ad campaign for an airline, it was the articulation of a real ambition for a nation. HerdBuoys McCann stated and demonstrated through this work all of the hopes and desires for what South Africa could and would become. I will never forget it.

Partnering with a Pioneer

Real ambition was again the engine at work during a time of enormous change at Unilever.

When I was at Interpublic I was asked by the holding company's CEO, Michael Roth, to go see a guy named Tony Wright, chairman of Lowe Worldwide, one of the Advertising Agency companies of Interpublic. Michael warned me by telling me that Lowe's main client, Unilever's global laundry detergent brand, Omo, had been put in review. To lose this business would be to effectively shut the agency. Big stakes. I met up with Tony, a great guy and a brilliant strategist who became my partner in crime when I later joined Lowe. Lowe was disadvantaged in every possible way: It was a smaller, disjointed patchwork of agencies pitching a global business against established behemoths. The odds of success were not great.

Our hidden agenda work was based on real ambition. We judged our new clients to be far-reaching visionaries who saw the need for wholesale change in the way marketing communications were undertaken. We could see clearly that they planned to bring sweeping changes and modernization to the Unilever marketing organization. One of the key requests in the initial briefing was that the agency put forward its view of what a twenty-first-century agency would look like.

The hidden agenda: We want to be pioneers of new marketing pathways.

The pitch took place in two stages, with the first an articulation of what the organization of the twenty-first-century agency would look like. Some weeks later, we met to demonstrate that agency in action. Our first presentation, scheduled to take no more than an hour, was a sweeping indictment of current agency design, and introduced a bold new language of idea communities, amoeba-like organizational design, and the like. We scored well, but the true test would come in a month's time.

The second phase was a test of the agency's ability to articulate the global and important regional interpretations of the brand platform "Dirt Is Good," an imaginative marketing approach based upon a belief that children develop through play, often messy play. This second phase required an elaborate coordination of presentations in each of four regions, tied to a final presentation at the offices of each of the participating agencies. The template and language of the agency we promised to create was put into practice in each of the regional meetings, so that the formerly disjointed Lowe now appeared like a cohesive twenty-first-century global unit. The real magic was the final show.

We decided that in order to give the Unilever executives a real sense of imaginative and collaborative power found in our central team and those four regional subteams, we would assemble each as a living demonstration of the way the team would work, at our location over the course of their three-hour visit. The client was ushered into a simple conference room where the central team made the opening strategic presentation. Doors swung open at the back of the conference room, where a starting gate, like the ones used in track and field events, had been assembled. The gate led out of that conference room and into the remainder of the agency. Ushered onto the roof of the building, the client team entered a gallery-like construction designed to house each of the four regions and the management teams, to exhibit a spirited cultural celebration and piece-by-piece articulation of the multidisciplinary program that would be explored for "Dirt Is Good" in each region. We in fact hired one of our sister companies, Jack Morton, the folks who staged the Olympic Games in Athens, to construct the gallery. It was breathtaking.

Tony Wright observed, "The challenge was to show how an idea would work across multiple markets, with culturally significant local ideas but to retain a global thought. It was a new model, a hugely ambitious client in one of the toughest categories with multiple agendas. How to partner a pioneer in a new way was the hidden agenda we uncovered."

It was a tight race, but this landmark presentation stabilized the business for Lowe. And, over the next few years Lowe became the largest single agency for Unilever worldwide.

The Elements of Real Ambition

"We choose to go to the moon in this decade and do the other things, not because they are easy, but because they are hard, because that goal will serve to organize and measure the best of our energies…"

—*John F. Kennedy*

Real ambition is not a *hope for*, it is a *will be*. It is the objective that growth aspirants identify and pursue relentlessly. It is what spurs a nine-year-old like I was toward a burning desire to make my mark with Henry Higgins–like diction, or spurs men like Dimape, Peter, and Happy, born in a South African township, to build a company in a new, inclusive nation. The real ambition is something everyone in your organization should be able to recite. It drives all of the individual activities in and around the organization. *Real ambition* has five key qualities:

It has noble intentions. The real ambition must serve an overarching goodness. It must be of benefit to all constituencies, both in and outside of the organization. Your real ambition is the compass that guides all of the activities of this citizenship. The real ambition appeals to the core in all of us that wishes to be a part of creating something special.

It is a statement of clear intent. Real ambition is not a destination or a "hoped for" goal. It is a steely confidence in what is to come. It is a statement of unequivocal intention and certainty of purpose that cascades to all corners of the organiza-

136

tion and makes it clear that almost is not good enough and half measures are no measures at all.

It seems impossible. Real ambition is not about increments or percentage points. It's about a great leap to a completely new state of being. No matter what role they play in the company, people want to be part of a vitally important journey toward a landmark achievement, especially that which no one thought possible.

It has a catalytic core. Real ambition has a core emotional content that is its fuel. Real ambition requires action, and the catalyst for that action is not transaction, it is belief. It is a belief in something collectively embraced and wholeheartedly pursued. It fuels courage and, by its very essence, it causes change and mobilization. It should not inform or state. Real ambition should motivate, stir, inspire, and galvanize.

It's in simple human language. The real ambition must be understandable from the grassroots foundations to the heights of the boardroom. Its language must be such that it can reach the hearts of everyone, at every level. The real ambition statement is the wellspring of your pitch. This crucial starting point is the locus around which you and your organization revolve. It is a mutual agreement among the community that is your organization. From the board member to the guy who moves the furniture, everyone must be conscious of this real ambition, because each effort, however large or small, is vital to making the ambition a reality. As a consequence, the real ambition statement must be an inspired, emotive, and inspirational piece of prose. Yet many fall short. I have seen all too many of these try hard, but fall prey to business speak. I wrote one for fun and illustration:

> *Company A: To be an innovator in our product development and delivery in our category developing technological strategies and solutions that anticipate customer demands and needs in the marketplace.*

Oh, boy. This statement is cluttered and vague, and it uses stiff, complicated language and boardroom clichés. It is lacking in emotion and any element of human motivation. It is hard to imagine how this statement affects life on the factory floor, or how the whole company citizenship should feel about its future. Would you want to work for this company? With the help of a bit of imagination and some work on a real ambition statement, it might now read:

> *Company A will be a pioneer that creates technological leaps for people's most precious needs, because of a belief that scientific advancement is a gift in the service of humankind.*

Wow! This is inspired. It is confident, pure, and simple in intent. It is catalytic and motivating. It is a crystal clear ambition and it implies how one might contribute to something that feels like a movement. Want to work for Company A now?

 ## Okay, Here's How

Developing a real ambition, like finding your core, is about reaching deeply within. All of us have harbored a longing from our earliest moments. For me, sitting in front of that radio as a child drove a desire to someday find myself in those far-off places living a global life. Somehow, the older we get, the more our ambitions and desires are tempered by what we think of as the practical realities of achieving them. When you're looking deeply at your real ambition, try to become eight years old again. Put aside for the moment the practical considerations. Establishing a real ambition for HerdBuoys McCann to have a role in South Africa's unity and for MasterCard to surpass Visa as the card of choice have one thing in common: They seemed utterly impossible.

With this in mind, take some time to create your real ambition. Do so only within the context of *what you wish it to be*. Take out a sheet of paper and answer the following questions for both you and your organization. They will stimulate your thinking about your real ambition:

What was I put on earth to do?
What is the best job I could ever have?
If I had every resource at my disposal, what would I set out to do?
What will I want people to say about me or my company?
How will others benefit from my (or our) special abilities?

The Real Ambition Statement

When you write a real ambition statement, you should feel nervous. Advancement in your life and your career means reaching for and doing things that you've never done before. When you're standing still and know every aspect of what you're doing there is no reason to feel nervous. Doing things you never did before *should* bring you the jitters. When I was first made a senior vice president at McCann I called upon a mentor of mine named John Fitzgerald, someone I had long admired. I told him I was terrified. I admitted I actually had no idea what to do. "I'm terrified," I confessed. "You are supposed to be," he said. " If you're not, you're not growing."

The real ambition statement that you create should inspire you and should be able to inspire others. It should be an honest and accurate reflection of what you *will* accomplish. If at the same time it makes you just a little bit nervous about the real ambition journey you are about to embark on, then you know it's right.

Now, I confess that the South African Airways example I shared, as well as many of the others, were very intuitive experiences. Later I realized that the process could be made more purposeful if we used a simple tool, which I'm calling the real ambition statement. A version I learned while a pup working on General Foods business went like this:

To____*[target audience]*____, ____*[brand name]*____ is the
____*[frame of reference]*____ that ____*[point of difference]*____ .

I remember one from my training:

To concerned coffee drinkers, Sanka is the brand of coffee that has no caffeine to upset you.

Each of the elements is there:

Target audience: Concerned coffee drinkers
Brand name: Sanka
Frame of reference: Coffee
Point of difference: No caffeine to upset you

We used these statements to debate amongst ourselves the positioning elements; for example, should the element be "coffee" or "beverage," and the like. The brilliance of this tool was its simplicity. It was structured with recognizable elements—*target audience, frame of reference,* and *point of difference*—that needed to be discussed and decided upon.

To aid in the discussion and decisions surrounding your real ambition, let's take a page out of the positioning statement exercise, but with a few modifications. With the key qualities outlined earlier, the real ambition statement has two key components.

The transformational element: This is the core of the real ambition, a state of being; it's the transformed entity that the growth aspirants of the organization seek. This is the component of the ambition that is far-reaching and wholly game changing.

The noble intent: This is the element of the real ambition that raises the stakes and gives it a motivating purpose (inspired by my friends at M&C Saatchi).

Putting it together looks like this:

[Organization] will be _[transformational element]_ that _[noble intent]_ .

Looking back at the real ambition that Peter, Happy, and Dimape envisaged and agreed upon in a living room in South Africa, it was clear that, while the statement was intuitive, its essential elements had been discussed and effectively agreed upon by the three men. So, with a little poetic license and a little after-the-fact authorship, a real ambition statement for HerdBuoys might have looked like this:

HerdBuoys will be a role model of unity and excellence for the new South Africa, and represents what our country can become.

Here are the elements:

Transformational element: Role model for excellence and unity
Noble intent: Represents what our country can become

I sent it to Peter, Happy, and Dimape. They approved.

Apartment 15B

Less than ten years after Rudy Giuliani and his team took office, against all conventional wisdom the "City on a Hill" had become the "*Shining* City on a Hill." Times Square, once a center for violent crime, was now a center of entertainment and enjoyment. Where murderers and shakedown artists had once roamed now roamed New Yorkers enjoying an evening out and enthusiastic visitors from all over the world, the very people who had once stayed away because they were too frightened. Crime rates dramatically reduced, welfare rolls were reduced by one half, and the economy was thriving. This result, and the entire organizing principle behind New York City's renaissance, was driven by a clear and unmistakable real ambition, an unswerving credo, and the core of a man who moved a city and a nation.

Once Rudy became mayor, I stayed close to the administration. I would bring the resources of McCann (with their enthusiasm) to assist with city programs, whether it was with research or ad campaigns. One project in particular stands out above all others.

While crime had been trending downward for some time, there was still a serious challenge to motivate citizens to report crimes, even when they represented threats to life and limb. The reason: The reports went to the local precinct. Callers would be asked their names and addresses. Now, while a caller's identity was, of course, protected, many would not call for fear that their names might somehow be revealed and that they would suffer reprisals.

An anonymous, toll-free number and reporting system was established, completely confidential. The caller didn't have to give a name. The system was linked to a special response team, called TNT, set up by the police department. The team would respond to drug-dealing gangs, many of whom would escape detection by forcibly taking over apartments in public housing projects. The residents were terrified. We developed an ad campaign that ran all over the city, to introduce this new phone line. Responses went through the roof, with hundreds of calls a week. The real impact, though, was shared with me by a police officer on the mayor's security detail.

It seems that a call came into the hotline and a TNT team was dispatched to a housing project in the Bronx, where a drug-dealing gang was doing brisk business. Imagine this: For the residents, there were daily threats from the gang and shady people coming and going at all hours. The NYPD took out the gang, arresting them all in one swoop.

The sergeant on the scene, while taking one final check as he walked through the hall after it was all over, was stopped as a door slowly opened. It was apartment 15B, down the hall from where the gang held forth. An elderly resident looked out tentatively, stepped out, approached the sergeant, and whispered, looking him in the eye, "Bless you." She disappeared into her apartment as quickly as she appeared. No more was said. It was more than enough.

A real ambition for a city, found in 15B.

The formation of a clear, seemingly impossible real ambition is a badge of courage for the growth aspirant who leads an organization. The *"It will be done"* attitude that is at the core of real ambition and its noble intent is essential in creating your pitch. It lays out for everyone you encounter a clear and unequivocal point of view and an expression of what you seek to do. It is the first and most vital step in creating your pitch.

Well, it's decades later, and I am still seated in front of that radio. My grandfather gave it to me for my birthday when I turned sixteen. It has been with me ever since, a prized possession and a symbol of all my lifelong aspirations. It has crossed the ocean with me to London, where I now live happily. The radio, by the way, still works, but I have to go now...Brahms' Piano Concerto No. 1 is on BBC 3, must turn it up.

And Now...

Now that we have a clear understanding of the hidden agenda, what it is and how to connect to it, let's look at how to ignite your audience through the clarity of your thoughts and the inspiration of your message, your *win strategy*.

REMEMBER THIS

Real ambition is the human desire to create some-thing good where nothing existed before. It is a measure of your worth, and of the worth of your organization. It's a key element of what inspires people to follow you. Real ambition is your own fiery desire to grow, to go from one state to an expanded one. Real ambition is the engine of your pitch. It is a never-ceasing quest that drives growth aspirants toward a special "place." Pursuit of real ambition provides all-important direction for any pitch.

PART III

HOW? SPEAKING TO THE HIDDEN AGENDA

7

Your Win Strategy

. . . .

Winning occurs when a shared bond is created with your audience through connecting your leverage-able assets—your real ambition, your credo, or your core—to your audience's hidden agenda.

In moments of exasperation, my mother could be heard to say, "When they were handing out brains, you missed the announcement!" Actually, she was and is my greatest fan, but I could be a thoroughly exasperating child. Apart from my exhausting persistence (key element of a pitchman, though...), I was a bit, well, absentminded. I am happy to say, though, that when *human instinct* was given out, I was lucky to be at the head of the line. Human instinct wins business and creates followings. Discipline, however, is a critical ingredient, too. Having a process and a structure for creating your pitch ensures nothing is left to chance. This is a lesson I had to learn.

The Leverageable Asset

Your core, credo, and real ambition are what I call *leverageable assets*. They are the means by which you bond with your audience. This is the moment of truth, more important than any other step in the process, because the insights that you have gleaned into the hidden agenda of your audience is the foundation upon which your approach is based. *This simple distillation of the human desire you have observed about your audience determines which leverageable asset you will bring to bear and the manner in which you will frame the brief, arrange your team, and shape the story, and it influences the ultimate outcome.*

One of the greatest pitch tragedies I have witnessed, and which I still see, is when an earnest team takes a brief at face value, charges forth, works slavishly, and presents with conviction their best professional solution. They wait with bated breath and then find themselves disappointed. How could this happen, after so much hard work, when they had what they thought was the right answer? *It is because the right answer lies not in the technical solution alone, but in its reflection of the win strategy you have hatched...the connection of your leverageable asset to the hidden agenda.*

A Method to the Madness

I mentioned earlier that I was a bit of an "odd man out" at McCann. It was very much a finance-driven, process-oriented culture ("script" profile, clearly). As you can imagine, at a company of this profile with 205 offices to manage, there was no shortage of procedure, tools, and practices, along with widely understood language, designed to help the ship run smoothly.

When we began the process of transforming the company, the first task I had was to show my colleagues that winning business and creating a following was every bit as strategic as what went on in the finance department. They blanched. I think they had visions of business cards printed with "Director of Emotional Occurrences," and I'm sure it sent their blood pressure rising.

Winning organizations are those that recognize the hidden agenda as the emotional driver behind every decision and institutionalize this all-important process as they would any other process in the organization. *Every turnaround I have participated in, every new business pitch I undertook, every audience I pursued was driven in no small measure by the institutionalization of the search for the hidden agenda.* I have learned that companies that win consistently and foster a robust and growing following do so as a direct consequence of methods, practices, and language that are widely understood. Creating these things becomes as natural to the organization as creating a balance sheet.

I came across a fabulous saying when I started my company: *If I had more time, I'd have written a shorter letter.* An awful lot of people have claimed to have said that, including Mark Twain and Cicero. All I know is, I love it and it suggests one of the most important and profound skills necessary for winning a business and creating a following: *distillation.*

There is another key belief, actually more a way of life, espoused by one of my very first clients, a remarkable group called M&C Saatchi. This multinational marketing communications company boasts accounts like Google, Pernod Ricard, Siemens, Nokia, and Qantas Airways, to name but a few. It was founded by the legendary Maurice and Charles Saatchi, along with several others, including a compelling guy named Moray MacLennan, the company's CEO. I have had the great delight of working with these folks and seeing the company grow through a fundamental belief in what they call "Brutal Simplicity of Thought." They have a very simple argument, outlined in a simple three-part piece of logic:

Brutal Simplicity of Thought

It's easier to complicate than to simplify.
Simple ideas enter the brain quicker and stay there longer.
Brutal simplicity of thought is therefore a painful necessity.

The people at M&C Saatchi rightly believe that wisdom is found in distilling a set of issues down to a single, clarifying, motivating thought. This is very hard work, but it's work that pays dividends. They further developed a simple yet profound framework (a tool, if you will) for developing their thinking to get to the Brutally Simple Thought. They call it three-box thinking, and here it is:

The Equation

It looks simple, but don't let looks deceive you. It is no mean feat to not only get the answers to those little sentences right, but to make them profound. What's important is that the three-box equation provides a commonly accepted means of moving forward and a language based on a belief of what it takes to win and create a following, institutionalized for all. Tools are not prescriptive; they are a good means of organizing common sense. They are especially good for bringing your team together around a process all can share. So, perhaps in a quest for the hidden agenda, and inspired by simplicity, we could use a tool, too.

Distilling with the Allen Key

I am an inveterate tinkerer. I love to open up my toolbox on a glorious Saturday morning and set about to make the world a better place through my handiwork. (Sadly, many of the tasks I set forth on end with a phone call to a pro, but we won't dwell on that.) In my toolkit is an unusual little tool called an Allen key. It's not as common as a screwdriver. It has a hexagonal shape and is bent like an "L." This highly specialized little tool can only unlock a special screw.

It occurred to me one Saturday morning, as I was unscrewing a light fixture with this special tool, that there was no better analogy or terminology to describe the special means of unlocking the hidden agenda and your leverageable assets than the Allen key. (It also did not hurt any that it just happened to have my name....) Here it is:

The Allen Key is designed as a reference guide to bring all the essential elements of your win strategy together. It will assist you as you consider the options and make your decisions regarding the final hidden agenda you determine and the leverageable asset you apply to deliver on it. It's important to remember that so much of this is an instinctive human endeavor. My goal in fashioning this simple tool is to give you a framework that you and your colleagues can use while brainstorming about the hidden agenda and how you will connect with it. When you're tinkering with your win strategy, it helps to have a handy tool. I hope this one helps you.

Connecting to the Hidden Agenda

The *win strategy* is the connection of one of your *leverageable assets* to the *hidden agenda* you have uncovered. Each of your leverageable assets—real ambition, credo, or core—is a means to unlocking one of the three elements—wants, values, or needs—of the hidden agenda:

The *real ambition* is used to connect to the *want,* because of the vision shared by you and your buyers of what the future will become. You are joined because they see that their ambitions are possible with you.

The AllerKey

Prospects Hidden Agenda

Values

Wants

Needs

Core

Real Ambition

Credo

Your Leveragable Assets

154

The *credo* is used to connect to the *values*, because together they form a belief system you and your buyers share. You are joined because you best understand them.

The AllerKey

The *core* is used to connect to the *need*, because there is something special you have that solves what your buyers lack. You are joined because they see you have the solution.

The AllerKey

Looking back at some of the pitches outlined in earlier chapters, here's how leverageable assets aligned to the hidden agenda were revealed:

The Hidden Agenda	The Leverageable Asset

MasterCard

"We need to score a victory over Visa in the marketplace and in doing so be famous for it...but the odds are stacked against us." ➤ **Core:** *McCann's competitive culture and winning track record.*

South African Airways

"We want to be sure we do the right thing, because the eyes of the world are upon us." ➤ **Real Ambition:** *HerdBuoys' genuine reflection of South African unity and aspiration.*

Marriott International

"We value the importance of being at the cutting edge of the lodgings industry, but do not want to compromise our values in the process." ➤ **Credo:** *A culture built around the honor and nobility of service—the "Spirit to Serve."*

The Process

Connecting with the hidden agenda—a largely intuitive process—essentially gives you license to factor emotion and human desire into the development of your win strategy, wrongly assumed to be based exclusively on cold hard facts. *The difference is consciously institutionalizing this intuitive process for every pursuit, every time.* In fact, every human being has the ability to empathize, to follow his instincts, and to form emotional bonds with another person. Think of these things as exercise: you need to develop new muscles and keep them toned. I have to say that it is often the case that a winning pursuit aligns on two or all three elements. There is no mistaking however, that there is a driving force behind it all, and why I urge you to focus on selecting the single most compelling answer.

Remember, the Brief Is Not the Brief

Very often when we are confronting a new business opportunity or the goal of creating a following, we first encounter the technical assignment. This assignment might include things like "increase market share," "drive sales performance," "meet and exceed sales targets," "recruit new members," "mobilize swing voters," and so on. This is the rational starting point. It is even described as the objective for the mission. *I say this is neither the mission nor the objective. Rather, the assignment is the means by which the hidden agenda will be realized.* The real mission is the *hidden agenda* at the heart of your target. The key is unlocking it and driving the task through the motivation of the hidden agenda you have identified.

The Importance of Language

I found that the way to institutionalize fresh thinking in organizations was through the creation and consistent use of language linked to a program. So when I say *win strategy*, *hidden agenda*, *credo*, *core*, and *real ambition*, people know exactly what I'm talking about. This requires evangelizing, and a lot of it. I would assemble my success stories and effectively communicate them to people inside my organization so they could tie the new terms to business success. It wasn't hard to create a following inside my organization as a consequence. After all, people love to win, and language that is associated with winning is well worth adopting (actually, it spreads like wildfire.)

Of course the process must also be institutionalized, and a special session called the *win strategy meeting* is an invaluable means of introducing a new kind of session. After all, there are all kinds of meetings, like budgeting and forecasting meetings, so why can't there be one that marks the pursuit of business or the creation of a following?

The Win Strategy

Once you have done your digging and completed your interviews, and after a good deal of soul searching, you can set about distilling the win strategy process (with Allen Key at the ready) down to three key steps:

1. **Uncover** the hidden agenda, the emotional desire at the core of what motivates your customer. Decide whether it is a want, a need, or a value.
2. **Select** from your real ambition, credo, or core. One of these will best satisfy the emotional need locked in the hidden agenda. Think of each of these as part of your toolbox; one of these will be best suited for reaching and answering the needs of the hidden agenda.
3. **Marry** the formal "task" given to you at the outset of your pursuit to the hidden agenda.

The Win Strategy Meeting

If there are a few of you who are stakeholders in the process, assemble your core team for a *win strategy meeting*. At this session a very special dialogue will ensue. Be sure you have all those who will play a part in crafting your approach, as this is where you will connect your leverageable assets to the hidden agenda you have uncovered and drive your response. If you are creating the strategy on your own, why not put a few people from your "board of directors" together—the sparring partners will do you good, I assure you.

The Win Strategy Statement

A creative director once told me, "Give me the freedom of a tightly defined strategy!" The win strategy statement is a summation and motivating force behind your pursuit. It becomes your blueprint for all the activities your team does in its preparations. The win strategy statement is a crisp distillation of how you are going to fulfill the emotional needs of your buyer, so as to connect with the hidden agenda. It has two simple parts: the hidden agenda and the selected leverageable asset you have chosen.

Here is a template:

The win strategy for _____*[audience]*_____ is to connect _____*[your leverageable asset]*_____ with _____*[their hidden agenda]*_____ .

For example:

The win strategy for <u>MasterCard</u> is to connect <u>McCann's winning spirit and competitive track record</u> with <u>MasterCard's concern that it will be a challenge to surpass Visa.</u>

Win Strategy Summaries

As a last step, assemble your complete win strategy on a single sheet of paper. This strategy includes the hidden agenda, the leverageable asset you have chosen to exercise, the win strategy statement, and notes on how you will tie these things to the functional brief you have been given. The following pages offer a summary of the key pitches I described earlier, targeting the hidden agenda with each of the three leverageable assets, summarized by a win strategy statement. If you can distill your pitch down to these essential elements, you are on your way to winning. Here are win strategy summaries for a few of the pitches I have discussed so far, one for each of the three leverageable assets.

WIN STRATEGY SUMMARY: *MasterCard*

The AllerKey

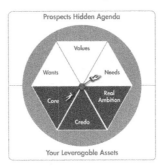

Hidden agenda: *We need to score a victory over Visa in the marketplace and in doing so be famous for it … but the odds are stacked against us.*

Intensive interviewing revealed MasterCard's deep desire to win over Visa and to be recognized for it, along with concern amongst the team as to whether Visa's dominance and deeper pockets could ever be overcome.

Core: McCann Erickson was well known for its combative corporate culture and instinctive competitiveness, as well as for its penchant for winning one-on-one brand battles (Coke versus Pepsi, AT&T versus MCI). This winner's attitude (and competence) would be targeted to MasterCard's ambition to become winners, besting Visa in the marketplace for the first time in fifteen years.

Win Strategy Statement: Connect McCann's cultural orientation toward winning and its inherent self-confidence with the hidden agenda of MasterCard's desire to best Visa in the marketplace once and for all.

WIN STRATEGY SUMMARY: *Marriott International*

The AllerKey

Hidden agenda: *We value the importance of being at the cutting edge of the lodgings industry, but do not want to compromise our values in the process.*

The belief that there is honor and nobility to be found in excellent service goes to the heart of Marriott's culture and to the teachings of the company's founder, J.Williard. Marriott. This was the lens through which Marriott would judge any recommendation.

Credo: Demonstrate the parallel value system of customer centricity and a deep appreciation for Marriott International's corporate culture from the very first solicitation to the pitch recommendation itself.

Win Strategy Statement: The win strategy for Marriott was to connect the company's abiding belief in the nobility of service with McCann's culture of client centricity and its intimate understanding and expression of Marriott's own credo.

WIN STRATEGY SUMMARY: *South African Airways*

The AllerKey

Hidden agenda: *We want to be sure we do the right thing, because the eyes of the world are upon us.*

In the first few years of post-apartheid South Africa, the airline knew that great importance would be placed on how and what it communicated; South African Airways was seen as reflective of this new nation, and the decision-making panel felt the weight of this responsibility.

Real ambition: HerdBuoys McCann, the first black South African advertising agency, connected to South Africa Airways via their own real ambition to become a symbol of the new South Africa by virtue of their African roots and the agency's diversity.

Win Strategy Statement: Connect HerdBuoys McCann, genuine reflection of South African unity and aspiration with the hidden agenda and the pressure decision makers at the airline felt to reflect the new South Africa successfully.

And Now...

With your strategy firmly in hand, it is time for you to craft a compelling argument. Let's take a page out of a court-room drama and make an ironclad case through the *advocate's approach*. Counselor, you may proceed...

REMEMBER THIS

. . . .

The *win strategy* is the connection of your leverage-able assets to the hidden agenda. The particular desire you have observed in your buyer determines which leverageable asset you will bring to bear and the manner in which you will frame the brief, arrange your team, and shape the story, and it will determine the ultimate outcome. This decisiveness forms the foundation for your argument.

8

The Advocate's Approach

· · · · · · · · · · · · · ·

Your argument is the creation of an ironclad theorem that logically supports the hidden agenda. It is the superstructure of your pitch.

It was at McCann that my early training advanced a great leap because of another extraordinary fellow, one of my cherished mentors, Peter Kim. Soon after the disaster of the Coca-Cola loss, the CEO of McCann Erickson elected to bring in some new talent, starting with Peter as Worldwide Vice Chairman and Executive Director of Strategic Planning. Peter had been a wunderkind at J. Walter Thompson, becoming an Executive Vice President of Strategic Planning for the company in his late twenties. But that was nothing. Peter graduated college at eighteen, immediately entered the Ph.D. program, and was an instructor at New York University at nineteen! South Korean by birth and the son of an international South Korean businessman who emigrated to the United States, Peter came from a family of super achievers—his sister won a full scholarship to Julliard to study the piano at the age of nine—he was probably the greatest business winner I ever encountered. He believed you win through the "crushing weight of logic." Peter once told me, "You don't have to be the biggest guy in the room to overwhelm."

No one could create and deliver a pitch quite like Peter. He would seize his audience, carrying them on a journey of crushing logic to an irrefutable conclusion. I can't recall a time when he did not leave his audiences dazzled. It was magic to watch. Peter believed in careful sequencing: a powerful and exacting opening, a careful recitation of evidence, and an irrefutable summation. It was an invaluable lesson.

The Litigator

I like to think of the pitch not as a presentation but as an important case being argued in a court of law. As a kid, I used to watch *Perry Mason*, a television courtroom drama in which Perry invariably won his case. It seemed that in virtually every episode there was an opening scene where Perry leans on the railing, looks at the jury, and says with gravity, "Ladies and gentlemen of the jury, I will prove beyond a shadow of a doubt that my client could not have committed the murder because he was not there!" The drama unfolds and evidence, anecdotal and factual, is presented as exhibits A, B, C, and so on. Then, in a swirl of drama, Perry Mason delivers an impassioned close, showing that "My client should be set free because, as you have seen from the evidence, he is an innocent man!" This is precisely how an effective pitch is organized: with a powerful, themed opening that directly reflects the hidden agenda, a crisply organized recitation of evidence, and a compelling, irrefutable summation.

To understand this phenomenon and technique, I spoke

with my friend Denny Young, who I interacted with when he was Chief Counsel to Rudy Giuliani. Prior to that, Denny had been Deputy United States Attorney when Rudy was United States Attorney for the Southern District of New York. He spoke of the techniques of being a litigator, reeling off phrases like "preponderance of evidence," "burden of proof," and "beyond a reasonable doubt." He talked about putting forward a comprehensive argument he called the "flow of logic." He urged me to spend some time looking at the techniques of litigators, and the next day I found myself amid stacks of law books dealing with this fascinating subject. When I was asked as a kid what I wanted to be when I grew up, I always replied, "a lawyer." So I was in seventh heaven poring over these wonderful books.

Making Your Case

The first thing I found in common among the fine authors of the law texts I studied was the importance they place on the clarity and singularity of the argument. This is the tough part, but it is the crux of any legal case. To be understood, for people to grasp what you're saying and to follow your argument, you must be as clear as you are compelling. The magic in the *advocate's approach* lies in compelling clarity that comes from crystal clear logic. This is a critical reduction to an essential core that can be shared and understood by virtually all communities. Creating a logical argument is a step the majority avoids. As a result, most pitches are cluttered, unclear, and lacking in motivation. It is an act of courage to decide in favor of a single theory for your "case." It's hard. It requires a brutal decisiveness, and this is a key skill that separates the winners from those who fall short. The vital importance of a clear argument cannot be overstated. It is the structure around which your pitch is built.

Lawyers argue in two forms, the written brief and the oral argument. The first precedes the second. Generally, no oral argument is made unless a written one has been submitted to the court. I love this, because it reminds us that a winning presentation is based on painstaking preparation. A written brief requires discipline, and that the logic of the case has been painstakingly thought through. I have always believed that while the emotional intelligence involved in pursuit is paramount, it goes nowhere if it cannot be constructed into a persuasive, all-encompassing argument. I call it the *logic of emotion*. All of my legal books agreed on two very important elements for creating a compelling case: These are the *theorem* and the *structure of your argument*.

Your Theorem

The theorem is the narrative of your case. It is, in a few brief words, a unifying summary around which you present the issues and the supporting facts of your case. Litigators are urged to craft the theorem with the utmost of care. Every word is vital: they are cautioned not only to be economical in their use of words but to select them strategically. A litigator's statements should always be forceful and compelling.

When you think like a litigator, you first must identify your theorem. A theorem is your hypothesis. This is your view of what you believe the case is about and a compelling summary of what you want your jury to believe. So if we were Perry Mason, our argument might read something like this:

Ladies and gentlemen of the jury I will prove to you this is a case of mistaken identity and that my client did not commit the crime, because he was with his sainted mother all evening.

In the case that you are making to win a business or create a following, *the theorem is driven by the hidden agenda you have uncovered.* For our purposes, the theorem must crystallize how you have connected to the hidden agenda of your audience. This is the organizing principle of your case, and the one around which all of your facts and support are arrayed. Here is the theorem for MasterCard:

Carpe Diem
You see these words before you? They mean "seize the day." It is because this is your day...your time. You will stigmatize Visa's platform of conspicuous consumption and become the preferred card in customers' wallets, but most importantly in their hearts.

The Structure of Your Argument

Among all of the books I collected, noted among them was U.S. Supreme Court Justice Antonin Scalia's work *Making Your Case: The Art of Persuading Judges.* Key in his discussions were the role of the syllogism in the theorem and how much time and thinking should be invested in creating an effective syllogism. As Scalia notes, "If you have never studied logic, you may be surprised to learn—like the man who was astounded to discover that he had been speaking prose all his life—that you have been using syllogistic reasoning all along." (He was certainly speaking about Peter!) He goes on, "The victor will be the one who convinces decision-makers that his or her syllogism is closer to the case's center of gravity." Justice Scalia cited a structure for what he called a positive syllogism. I remember that in school my teachers called it the "if, then" sentence:

Major premise: All S is P.
Minor premise: This case is S.
Conclusion: This case is P.

Chief Justice Scalia argues that syllogistic logic is the most rigorous and therefore the most persuasive. He cites a simple syllogism:

Major premise: *A contract is not binding without consideration.*
Minor premise: *Johnson provided no consideration for this contract.*
Conclusion: *This contract is not binding.*

Looking back at the MasterCard experience, the syllogism might have looked like this:

Major premise: The value systems of "good revolvers" have become more inner-directed.
Minor premise: MasterCard's value systems are inner-directed.
Conclusion: The "good revolvers'" card is MasterCard.

From this core theorem, the litigator assembles the argument and hangs all of the evidence from it. It is through the crushing weight of logic, stemming from this theorem, that the litigator shows that the hypothesis is so.

A successful pitch requires speaking in the logic of emotion
  directed at the hidden agenda.
Strike this and you strike at the heart of your customer's desire.
Strike this desire, and you will win.

A good pitchman, like a good litigator, uses all the elements at his disposal: the real ambition, core, and credo, together with the hidden agenda at work. All of the elements combine with brutal clarity and persuasive logic. The *advocate's approach* drives your pitch through the hidden agenda around which your case is made. You win your case with a clear assertion of the hidden agenda and by presenting convincing evidence, your leverageable assets, to create an irrefutable reason why your audience should follow you.

Okay, Here's How...

When many organizations present a pitch, they often focus on a linear recitation of objectives, strategies, tactics, and the like, all in a nice, neat unconvincing sequence. The advocate's approach moves the presentation to a very different place, one of advocating for your point of view in no uncertain terms. The advocate's approach is compelling, moving, and should stir the audience. Remember, making a case is a whole lot different than reciting facts. A well-constructed case compels people to act, to believe, and to follow. Putting an argument together is a disciplined affair. Borrowing a page from our legal friends, I've made an outline you might find helpful. I use this logic flow to design every pitch I make, from those delivered at simple, informal, one-on-one meetings to those that entail bells-and-whistles extravaganzas.

The Opening Statement

This is a compelling recitation of your theorem in its purest and simplest form. It is a pithy, convincing summary, and the essence of your pitch. It must not be equivocal. It needs to make your case in no uncertain terms and articulate what is to be proven. *The opening statement is driven by the hidden agenda and your connection to it.* A good opening starts with, "I will argue that…"

Facts and Evidence

This is the process the legal folks call "discovery." It is a painstaking review of all the potential facts relevant to the case. For us, this is the search for the hidden agenda; it includes the things you have discovered in your meetings with the prospective client as well as the clues you've found that uncover the desire of your audience. Then it becomes a process of selecting the right pieces of "evidence" to make your case. Think of the pieces as "Exhibit "A," "Exhibit B," and so on. Rather than being a linear recitation, the presentation displays compelling proof of your connection to the hidden agenda.

The Logic Path

This is a roadmap for your audience that shows how you will set out to prove your "case." You can literally diagram the chain of your logic so that your audience will be clear about where you are taking them. Each of the elements at your disposal— the real ambition, core, and credo—and the hidden agenda all come together in crystal clear logic.

Summation

This is an explanation of the relationship between the facts and arguments that have been presented. It is a rousing summary of your "case" and what you believe your audience should do. The summation reinterprets your theorem, the hidden agenda upon which the pursuit rests, only this time it is woven with all the evidence and support you have presented as one coherent, compelling piece of logic.

The opening statement of the MasterCard pitch made it clear that now was MasterCard's time, because an opportunity existed that would vault MasterCard to leadership and fame. The evidence was spelled out, in compelling cadence: the shift to inner-directed societal values; the genuine core of MasterCard; and the conceptual target of "good revolvers," who believed they were buying good things for good reasons. The summation was put forward as a vision of the future, including a mock David Letterman skit of the "Top Ten Priceless" moments. Little did we know at the time that literally hundreds of "Priceless" spoofs (including some that cannot be printed here!) would one day race around the globe.

Your argument is a vitally important element in your successful pitch. It is the assembly and distillation of your point of view, and of supporting reasons to believe in your point of view, that you put forward to create your following. There is probably no greater test of the power of the advocate's approach than a pitch for a revolutionary product, from Johnson & Johnson.

Making the Case to ACT UP

I have always had a deep affinity with Johnson & Johnson. At a moment of injury, be it a scraped knee or a cut on the forehead, I was lovingly attended to by my mother and a

Johnson & Johnson Band-Aid. Johnson's Baby Powder and Shampoo seemed to be put on this earth to help people, to be gentle and caring and to reflect the love of family, in line with the company credo I shared earlier.

In 1998, while I was at McCann, Johnson & Johnson, one of our key clients, invited us to participate in a review for a developmental product. The intention: the first home-access HIV test ever created.

The product would be both a product and service. Consumers could purchase a simple, discreet kit, draw a sample of blood the same way they would to test for diabetes and the like, and send that card anonymously to a central Direct Access Diagnostics laboratory. A confidential phone number was provided, and trained counselors and support services were ready to assist callers with their results. It was a revolutionary concept for an unprecedented time, when testing was taboo and scaremongering rife. Irrespective of the test kit's controversy, McCann put its entire weight behind this effort. We knew what it meant to so many, and knew we had a responsibility to pursue and win this business.

The product was developed at a time when the root causes and treatment for AIDS were still being researched, amidst a growing belief that testing was the first key step in applying effective treatment. It was early days, and the stigma and fear surrounding the disease were enormous, as many did not believe that testing was the way forward. There were those who thought that testing was some sort of government plot to root out and persecute people with AIDS.

The hidden agenda: We need to know that your intentions are good.

Introducing the product was an incredible decision from the parent company, Johnson & Johnson. Amidst a swirl of controversy, the company believed in a product that, by definition, could help people profoundly. Early treatment saved lives, and this wonderful product could be a means of moving people into early treatment. Remarkable.

The Plain Truth

Our strategy for Confide rested on three key elements: our real ambition, the plain facts about testing, and Johnson & Johnson's credo. All other elements would be arrayed in support. Our real ambition was simple. We all believed in the product because people who got tested early could enter treatment. We would save lives. Second, the product, because of its 100 percent confidentiality, would assure people that they could test safely and anonymously. Finally, the key underpinning of Johnson & Johnson's credo would assure many skeptics that both the intention and the process were of the highest integrity.

I spoke earlier of Johnson & Johnson's credo. I remember going to the headquarters to take our brief and whiling away the time as we waited to be conducted to the offices. I stared at that piece of stone in Johnson & Johnson's corporate lobby, thinking carefully about what this credo meant. I reflected on what it meant for me as a nine-year-old with a scraped knee and what it meant for me now, as a person deeply committed to the AIDS issue and on the front lines for several years, about to pitch this momentous business.

The pitch team had been carefully selected, and many were

working on a volunteer basis, having joined us because of our dedication to the fight against AIDS. Many of us were actively involved in organizations on the battlefront, including me. Our excitement was real, for the introduction of this revolutionary product represented the weighing in of a major American corporation; it was a courageous act, and we were going to make sure this product succeeded. We conducted a thorough and effective pitch and were awarded the business. The real test, though, of the confidence in our pitch for Confide did not come until well after the Johnson & Johnson presentation, at a meeting of AIDS activists.

Into the Lion's Den

At a point well into the product development stage, marketing management at Johnson & Johnson decided that it would be important to engage with activists and opinion leaders in the AIDS movement. In doing so, they would be certain to get the buy-in and support of the frontline community, who up to this point had not been shy in their views. While getting this support was an important step, it was generally assumed that the product would be embraced wholeheartedly.

We arrived at a hotel and were shown into a very large conference room. A vast U-shaped table was populated by upwards of forty individuals, and another twenty-five or so were standing at the back of the room. It was not a happy mood. The marketing director began to speak, and I was positioned just behind him holding boards like some sort of game show hostess. After a few opening words of welcome, he turned the meeting over to me, saying, "Now I would like to ask Kevin Allen to speak about the program and the importance of the

Confide launch." I was stunned. I had expected only to hold boards aloft, not to face this formidable audience.

I stepped into the U-shaped arena, forming my words in virtually an instant. In a haze of nervousness, instinct somehow drove me back to the very simple core of our argument: Testing will stop people from dying. The other thing I thought of was the slab of stone. I reminded the audience of this massive wall, and, importantly what was written on it. I stated that we were put here on this earth to do good things for others, especially those who are in no position to help themselves. I believed that a moment had come when one of the world's great companies, Johnson & Johnson (whose own credo is a dedication to patients and those who love and assist them), could offer a means for helping people move away from the near certainty of a shortened life from the complications of AIDS.

The room exploded.

I have never seen more contorted faces nor angry outbursts in my life, yet somehow, because of what I felt to be true, rather than retreat I drove further into that U-shaped arena. I maintained steadily, over the pounding I was getting, an insistence on the importance of this product and the support of a singular company whose credentials in the area of doing the right thing were unassailable.

Not quite knowing what to do next, I turned to a woman on the panel who had an HIV testing site in California. I had chatted with her prior to the formal proceedings, and she had indicated to me her belief in the vital importance of testing and talked of the progress being made with individuals who were diagnosed early. I yelled for the group to hush, then turned the floor over to her, whereupon this soft-spoken yet passionate woman held the group spellbound with details of

177

her successes and why she believed there was no choice but to support this initiative. Her argument was simple: People are dying. Testing will save them. The commitment of Johnson & Johnson ensures the quality of the product. She spoke to the heart of the hidden agenda of everyone in the room, by recalling the spirit of Johnson & Johnson's credo. She asserted that everyone in the room had a "moral obligation to support this initiative," and she was quick to remind them that they might never get the support of a company like Johnson & Johnson again, so the time was now.

Just Testing

The conference came to a close with me, sweating and somewhat haggard, thanking the group and inviting them to the adjacent room for a cocktail gathering. Individual after individual, including some of the most noted AIDS activists in the country, acknowledged their support, each indicating that his attack was meant to ferret out the integrity of our intentions. They all agreed on the urgent importance of testing to society and that only Johnson & Johnson had the credo to overcome suspicions and concerns about this new product's integrity and efficacy. Thankfully, widespread testing quickly became a norm and I know in my heart that a special credo, from a special company, played a part.

Peter Passes the Torch

After strings of pitch successes, my mentor and friend Peter Kim decided to leave the company. His future was never in doubt, as he revealed to me during a pitch to AT&T in Washington. Over many chardonnays in Georgetown he revealed that he, like other members of his family, suffered from serious congenital heart disease. Peter told me, to my shock, that he would not live past forty. He was resolved to live his life completely and to pursue entrepreneurial aspirations that were at last entirely for him. This was something he richly deserved, after doing so much for so many, including me.

I remember this emotional conversation vividly; I asked him how on earth we would get by without him and told him how inadequate I felt to fill such immense shoes. He told me how important it was that all we had built continue, and with all his kindness said, "Don't worry, you'll do it in your own way, just be your own special self." There and then Peter reminded me, just as Ketchum chairman Bill Genge had so many years before, that a great pitch was about the courage and the strength to be yourself. As always, Peter's predictions were absolutely right. He tragically left this world at the turn of the millennium, aged forty years. Fact is, I never filled those shoes, not even a fraction. They were just too big. But the road he paved made the way for the team that went on to win over $2 billion in new business over the next few years, a team that included folks I've mentioned earlier as well as the formidable, yet good-hearted Eric Keshin, then head of McCann Erickson New York (later COO worldwide); the wonderful Nina DiSesa as Chairman and Chief Creative officer; Nat Puccio, who had been his best friend since their college days; and Suresh Nair, another brilliant strategic planner who is now the Global Planning Director for Grey Worldwide.

And Now...

With a clear and persuasive argument in place, it's time now to present your oral case. As one legal expert cited, your oral argument is a story of the issues at hand, and forms the crux of your case. Once upon a time...

REMEMBER THIS

Your *argument* is a vitally important element in your successful pitch. It is the assembly and distillation of your theorem and the supporting evidence that you put forward. Your argument is constructed on the foundations of syllogistic logic and is the structure around which your pitch is built. This critical reduction to an essential core is an act of courage; it requires that you decide in favor of the single core of who you are and what your organization is putting forward, excluding other possibilities.

9

The Power of Storytelling

· · · · · · · · · · · · ·

Storytelling, built around the hidden agenda, carries your audience with you through the power of
humankind's oldest and most motivating form of
communication.

The stage was set. The trio of strategists had laid down a car-
pet of brutal logic. Creative Director Jonathan, my friend and
a great talent, delivered the concept he envisaged, the core of
the pitch:

*There are some things money can't buy. For everything else
there's MasterCard.*

All the while, a small table sat amidst the enormous room
of McCann. On it was a large object with a linen cloth over
it. The linen was carefully pulled away, revealing a series of
books, three feet high, in royal blue velvet, with a small pol-
ished brass MasterCard logo elegantly affixed in the center.
The first book was opened carefully and the two brilliant cre-
ators of *Priceless*, Jeroen Bours and Joyce King Thomas, read

simple lines from a page of beautiful photographs of a father and son and in gentle tones:

Two tickets, $28
Two hot dogs, two popcorns, and two sodas, $18
One autographed baseball, $45
Real conversation with 11-year-old son...priceless

Speechless.

In riveting cadence, story after story expressing this brilliant idea was told, the most intense moment of the pitch and certainly for me, and for everyone in the room, of all our professional lives. The looks on the faces of the assembly told it all. They were spellbound. *It was because the pitch of this profound strategic thought was delivered in a time-honored means of communicating desire...storytelling.* All of the logic, all of the elements of the "case" were transformed into a story of longing, heroism, and attainment.

The MasterCard Story

While introducing the extraordinary recommendation for MasterCard, we told a story. This story was about a brand weak and vulnerable and a villain (Visa) with unbroken success, but it was also the story of a potential transformation. We offered MasterCard the power and control to turn the story around and allow MasterCard to take its rightful place as a winner in its marketplace. This was a story not of life as it is, but of how it could be. It was the outline of desire that we strongly believed we could achieve.

Storytelling is not communication. It is the delivery of passion, emotion, and desire. It has a singular ability to convey, motivate, and stir. Your pitch, to move from theorem and logic, must be woven into an audience-riveting story.

Storytelling is an inspired subject involving the human condition: heroes, villains, plot complications, struggle, journey, and redemption. Now, your pitch need not be Wagnerian, but nor it should be a mere recitation of fact; your pitch has to carry your audience with you by touching and moving them profoundly.

Once Upon a Time

Storytelling is as old as humankind itself. Scrawled on cave walls, told around campfires, read to one another by candlelight, or broadcast in living rooms and on the silver screen, tales of all types have been told throughout the ages. These stories were not merely recounting of events and activities. A story of hunting didn't go:

Uh, well, we went out, killed a wild boar, came home, and ate it.

Instead it was more likely to be:

We started early. It was a freezing morning and we felt the cold down to our bones. We moved along the trail, and as we did the thickness of the underbrush prevented us from seeing where we were going much of the time. Just then . . . a tiger appeared! We ran for our lives. As we ran, Ug tripped and fell down a ravine! Holding on for dear life, we formed a human chain and dragged him from certain death. All but one of my arrows fell to the floor below. We set out again, and before long we found a wild boar suddenly standing before us. He was enormous, and I knew we were in for a fight. Moving toward us, he charged. I raised my bow, reached for my last arrow, and let it fly . . . it was him or me. He leapt, and there in the tall grass we both fell, he with an arrow through his heart and I having secured the survival of our clan.

This wasn't a recounting of events but the tale of a quest, a setback, a daring feat, and a moment of triumph, as the hero attained what he set out for . . . food for the family. It has drama, excitement, and inspiration.

Storytelling first and foremost is a tale of desire. It chronicles a journey toward the attainment of a goal or the fulfillment of a wish. We all share desires, so the recounting of an exciting journey toward its attainment is a story everyone enthusiastically relates to. . . .*and listens to.* Through the ages, storytelling has been associated with truth and wisdom, and masterfully told tales have compelled audiences for generations. I'm a hopeless classic movie fanatic, so let's consider a few silver screen couples as examples. These characters inhabit love stories, most of them tragic, each one employing familiar elements designed to impart eternal truths and a good deal of wisdom:

West Side Story's *Maria and Tony: Love is eternal.*
Cleopatra's *Cleopatra and Marc Antony: Great love requires a sacrifice.*
Gone with the Wind's *Scarlett O'Hara and Rhett Butler: Passion alone does not love make.*

Each has a core theorem, just like we observed in our discussion of the *advocate's approach,* but this time it has an added layer of emotion and enduring human desire. For us this is the hidden agenda. At the root of the story is the core desire, both yours and that of your conceptual target.

Luck of the Irish

The most important thing a story does is make a human connection. I made mention earlier of my German roots. Well, I am sure you can tell that, with a name like Kevin, I have an awful lot of Irish blood in me, too. As you can imagine, pitching for the Irish Tourist Board's business held no small amount of significance for me. During the briefing process we could sense the clients' deeply held feelings about the country, which was struggling to evolve amidst violence; their love of country was clear in their view of the Irish people as unique in the world. I detected a self-consciousness about what they knew to be true about their country and the publicity surrounding the "troubles."

Their research was proudly shared with us, and it showed strongly that other worldwide destinations were places people visited to see significant things, but Ireland was a place people went to "participate." They enjoyed not only the beauty of the country but the spirit and openness of the people. Having a Guinness at a pub, joining a little sing-along at the bar, and myriad other means of engaging with the charming Irish people invited visitors to become a little "Irish" for a week or so. The research result was not only strategic but offered evidence to support the emotions of the Tourist Board client that we had detected in our early discussions.

Hidden agenda: We want people to experience the real Ireland. The warm, engaging spirit of the people who inhabit this

*beautiful place is the reason we're special. The publicity about
our country doesn't tell the real story.*

The presentation would take place, Dublin, and my role
was to open with our theme, found in the value system that the
members of the Irish Tourist Board and we ourselves held close:

*We believe this isn't just any destination pitch, because Ireland
isn't just any country.*

On the day of the presentation, I decided I would set the
stage by making a connection to this idea that Ireland was
more than just a country; it came as a result of a conversation
over dinner with my family two days prior to the pitch. My
opening went something like this:

"Good morning. Thank you so very much for having us.
I traveled a good distance to be here, as just this past
weekend I was with my mother and family in New York
for Easter. Over dessert I finally plucked up the courage
to tell Mom that I would have to travel to the airport and
so I would need to leave just after dinner."

"Airport? How could you? It's Easter weekend! What
on earth could possibly be so important that you would
leave today?"

"We're pitching the Irish Tourist Board."

"You get yourself on that plane this instant and if you
don't get it, don't come back!"

We all shared a laugh, but many in the audience may well have also heard their own mothers saying very similar things to them. Now, I could have said, "This presentation is very important to us, blah, blah, blah." Instead, employing a simple story, I found a context that underscored just how important this presentation was to us. The story showed our connection to people who felt the same about their beloved country. This human connection was made not only because we rightly understood what was emotionally important to our prospect, but because we used a simple story with familiar elements they could all relate to. It created a bond in an instant.

I am certain Grandpa Whalen, wherever he might be, was particularly proud of the fact that my colleagues and I had the privilege to work for the Irish Tourist Board for several years as a consequence of that wonderful pitch.

The Medium of Our Age

Of course, we have to ask, is all of this emotion and storytelling still relevant in the digital age? I say it is even more so. For a very long time, we lived in a world where people were dictated into action. We were told to comply, and to buy. Organizations firmly in control were fiefdoms with a select few telling and a good many complying. People were cajoled, persuaded, and convinced. The ideal businesspeople were hunters, aggressive and predatory, and the sale was a conquest. The conversation was...one-way.

We live in a new age. An age of community. A democratized world where people, "citizens," *opt in* and *choose to*, rather than being *told what* or *made to*. The most important news that anyone can hear in this new age is "So-and-so is following you." In this new world, you don't persuade anyone to do anything. It's not *buy* me, it's *join* me. You cannot demand your audience's attention. But you can ignite it through the time-honored practice of storytelling, which reaches into the heart of your audience's desire and connects profoundly to it. When you do this, people will follow you. They will embrace you and anything you represent, whether it is the direction of your company, the project you lead, or the product you sell.

Elements of the Story

He reflected how he had been persecuted and insulted, and now he was hearing everyone saying he was the most beautiful of all the beautiful birds. And the lilacs bowed down their branches into the water before him, and the sun shone so warm and so good. Then he rustled his feathers, raised his slender neck and cried out with a jubilant heart, "I did not dream of so much happiness when I was the Ugly Duckling."

Millions of children since 1843 have been told Hans Christian Andersen's story of inner beauty. Apparently a story reflecting Andersen's own life, "The Ugly Duckling" has been told and retold in dozens of languages the world over. It is a tale of overcoming the cruelty of judgment and the triumph of the beauty that lies within. In this charming story, and in every story, for that matter, there are a number of essential elements that can be called upon to create drama and to engage a shared sense of desire. Our ugly duckling was, of course, the hero, tormented for his ugliness by the villainous other little ducks. Throughout the long hard winter, the ugly duckling endured his bad fortune, until one day he transformed into a beautiful swan... *it's all there!*

Classic story structure is based on the *hero's journey.* It's wonderful. It is all about an individual who struggles to attain a goal. Obstacles get in the way, there are reversals, but in the end all impediments are overcome. Finally, a moral is told, the theme of the particular story in question.

Basic story construction has two components, the players and the journey.

As an illustration, let's make use of my very favorite film, *The Wizard of Oz. (Ok, it's my take on it!)*

The Players

The hero: The hero is the focus of our attention and the means through which the storyteller conveys the core theme. The hero in *The Wizard of Oz* is, of course, Dorothy. On a farm she sings of her dreams of a special place "over the rainbow." Every story has a hero (or "she-ro," as Maya Angelou would say). This is the individual everyone relates to and focuses on.

The villain: The villain is the opposing force, the element competing with and blocking the attainment of the hero's desire. Villains stir emotions and raise the stakes, creating drama and engagement. The Wicked Witch of the West, in all her greenness, does this beautifully.

The foil(s): These are characters who support the hero and, in particular, help to define the hero's character. The Tin Man,

Scarecrow and the Cowardly Lion, arrayed around Dorothy, help us see her character develop.

The sage: This is the person who offers wisdom for the hero along her journey. The Wizard, after being revealed as a humbug, offers each character a very special piece of wisdom. For example, to the Tin Man he says, "A heart is not judged by how much you love; but by how much you are loved by others."

The Journey

The journey that the hero sets out on has several key parts.

The quest: The quest establishes the goal that the hero seeks and sets the meaning and purpose for the journey. It is marked by many events along the way, adding to the drama as well as to the learning the hero experiences. The goal for Dorothy is to get back to Kansas, and the yellow brick road offers a vibrant symbol of the journey Dorothy sets out on.

Reversal of fortune: This is the moment of suspense when it appears our hero may not attain her goal. It is a moment when all seems lost and the outcome looks very much in doubt. This is when tension and drama grip the audience. Dorothy is imprisoned in the tower, Scarecrow is in pieces, and it seems to us that all is lost.

Turning point: The moment of truth. The tables turn and the hero is back on track. The melting of the Wicked Witch signals that Dorothy is released from evil and she regains the momentum of her journey.

Dénouement: This is the eureka moment, when the hero discovers what it is that can help her attain her desire. It's the summation of the story and it reveals the moral. With family and friends around, Dorothy exclaims, "I know that if I ever go looking for my heart's desire, I'll never go any further than my own backyard. For if it isn't there, I never really lost it."

The Hero's Journey

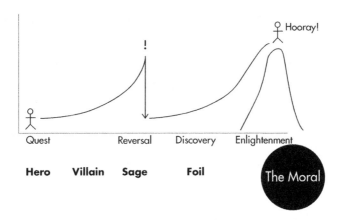

Now, whether you are a sentimental person, as I am, or a lover of film, as I also am, you will find the same essential elements of great storytelling in any number of tales: *Gone with the Wind, Star Wars, The Godfather: Part II,* or…your presentation!

May the force be with you.

Now, lest you think *storytelling* is ancient and has outlasted its usefulness, consider some angry birds, and some very bad pigs.

Angry Birds and Bad Pigs

I ran into a wonderful guy not long ago, Wibe Wagemans, who was on the selection team of a division of Nokia that I pitched in Finland a few years ago. We won the business and he and I stayed in touch over the last several years. He's now a key guy with a fascinating company called Rovio. They are a worldwide sensation and from my perspective a fantastic reflection of *storytelling's* enormous power. Among many ventures, Rovio set out to design a puzzle-based videogame. Their designers began with a *hero(s)*, a multicolored flock of little wingless birds. Quickly and instinctively, however, they realized that they needed a *villain*. Pigs were given this role and not just *any* pig...but green...and *bad*. Their whole lot in life is the perennial and shameless attempt to steal the little wingless birds' eggs! Villains!

Not taking this lying down, our *Angry Birds* have a quest, aided by the player who, using slingshots, hurls the Angry Birds at the *Bad Pigs* and their structures, a fitting justice for their predatory ways! Mikael Hed, CEO of Rovio Entertainment, observed that it is all about storytelling: "The unintelligent pigs, driven by their insatiable hunger and poorly developed instinct of self-preservation, are unable to pass up any chance of feeding on the delicious bird eggs. However, when the birds perceive their eggs to be in any kind of danger, they lose every shred of self-control and mental restraints they have, and will save no effort in securing the safety of their young." It's more fun than you can imagine.

Angry Birds has enjoyed broad appeal and engagement around the globe, importantly across a wide variety of ages (hmm...just like the ugly duckling) with a combined 300 million applications across all of their platforms having been downloaded. Film and television plans are afoot. The extraordinary worldwide following for *Angry Birds* created by some brilliant people from a little town in Finland was not by reason of the games technology on its own, but through the clever combination of brilliant game play and creativity, glued together through the use of the fundamentals of *story*. It's all there: the heroes of our *Angry Birds*, the evil villains in the *Bad Green Pigs*, the setbacks and triumphs, and the engaging role of the player in that story, all to make a decidedly fun and altogether delightful experience. Go get 'em *Angry Birds!*

The Moral of the Story

The central element of storytelling, what people relate to, is what happens to the heroes and the lessons that they learn. This is the "moral of the story," the takeaway. For our purposes, the hero is your audience. Your story is all about what your audience is striving to attain. The "moral" is the hidden agenda they seek, the unspoken desire they hold. Delivering your pitch persuasively means organizing your story around the hidden agenda of your audience, highlighting elements of the journey with drama. As you work to create your pitch, consider the elements of story as tools. Clearly, Visa provided a villain with which we could contrast MasterCard's genuine difference, but it also offered a focus around which Master-Card's emergence and transformation could be seen.

Why Story Is Compelling

Storytelling has a unique ability to address the hidden agenda. It does so because great storytelling rivets and inspires your following for several very important reasons:

Storytelling is genuine and authentic. Telling a story, just like our forebears did while sitting around a campfire, renders us completely and totally human. An endearing story is one in which, as I was once told, you "step out from behind the suit" and make an authentic connection with another human being. The reason that storytelling is so powerful is that this time-honored practice is understood as a means of connecting emotionally. This is its *power.*

Storytelling captures your audience's hopes. When you tell a story you bring your audience into a world that you create. You capture their imagination and invite them to visit and share, in the hope of creating a dreamt-of future. The story is motivating and inspiring and, of course, taps into what we have suggested drives human desire—hope. Your story suggests that the desire that resides in their hearts might be realized.

Storytelling offers drama. Unlike the exquisite and all-important logic outlined in the previous chapter, storytelling involves drama, passion, and surprise, all of which serve to engage. It is not possible to put yourself forward and make a profound connection if you can't find a means to engage with your audience. Facts do not move people. Remember, our legal friends were quick to point out that the oral argument is a story that weaves together all the legal facts in order to engage and persuade.

There are many examples I could give to illustrate the power of story, but probably the most compelling "case" was made in the pitch to an emerging new global brand from China Mobile.

There's Another Way

This is a real David and Goliath story involving a sparky little office of Lowe Worldwide in Shanghai. Our agency there consisted of a good group of about twenty-five people led by a fabulous lady named Kitty Lun. A real go-getter, Kitty secured us an opportunity in the first ever global brand launch, from China Mobile called Zong. Landing in Shanghai to assist the group, I remember arriving at the Regency Hotel, a very fancy place indeed. As I stepped out of the car and looked to my right, there, in a blaze of glory, was the huge logo of our competition (a five-hundred-person agency) emblazoned on a building with a Rolls-Royce dealership in the lobby. Oh boy.

A debrief with Kitty's team provided the usual background, which included China Mobile's strategy of introducing the brand around the world not to mature markets but to developing countries. After not a small amount of handwringing over the near certainty that the behemoth would be given the business, we had a realization that led to our conclusion about the *hidden agenda*: that while they had never introduced a brand outside China's borders before, we could sense that there was no appetite for imitation. Their desire was to chart their own path and be proud for doing so.

The Hidden Agenda: We want to make this launch a success and will be known for doing so in a new way.

This insight had at a dramatic impact on the way we would pursue the business. The natural inclination would be to try to "out-behemoth" our competition, to demonstrate prowess and global experience and to show how our vast experience would answer their need for a global communications partner. Against a formidable global competitor with a local powerhouse team, this did not seem viable. The answer came from an analysis led by an insightful and energetic guy named Cris Dawes. He uncovered a simple yet profound insight, that China Mobile simply because of its national origins shine as a beacon for developing market aspiration. Developing countries look to China because it shares much of the optimism and challenges of a developing economy (since much of that country is still in a state of development).

Putting aside a big global "show" with expansive case studies and other proofs of competency, our group instead selected five individuals from each of the countries where China Mobile planned to launch. Each of these young aspirants—from a street vendor in Kuala Lumpur to a young female lawyer in Pakistan—were interviewed at length. These people all told the stories of their lives and their struggles to become something better for themselves and their families. They didn't see themselves as "downtrodden." In fact, they saw themselves as people on the way up.

We showed China Mobile that they could succeed even without previous experience, because a real and profound connection with the aspirants in each of their respective targeted countries was truly the way to "go global" (*glocal*, actually).

As Cris pointed out, "China Mobile would become a global portal for human potential, empowering their aspirations and dreams rather than being the world's biggest phone company." The opportunity was not to embrace a global one-size-fits- all strategy, but to forge a shared bond with the ambitions of customers in each of their markets. This would ensure a positive impact for the brand. We reminded them through these wonderful individuals, who were so compelling in their stories, that ultimately all marketing is local. China Mobile would not become a faceless global brand applying well-worn; high-tech marketing idioms, but an empathetic company who embraces these individuals and the aspirations they hold close market by market. I can still feel the gnashing of teeth near the Rolls-Royce dealership when China Mobile decided to hire Cris, my dear Kitty, and her worldwide team.

Tone And Language

For so very long and to a large extent still today, the language of business has been the language of militarism: *objectives, tactics, missions, flanker brands*, and other terms from the language of war are used in everyday use in the conduct of business. I have lived it, as part of the "madman" culture of McCann Erickson. We saw ourselves as warriors and conquerors. Our battle cries were statements like, *"A marketing plan is a carefully designed plot to murder the competition"* and other pleasant ditties. Dreary stuff.

Ladies and Gentlemen Serving
Ladies and Gentlemen

A vitally important element in the crafting of your story is the appropriate use of language. The choice of language you use will set the tone for your organization and help you shape your business. A few years after we were awarded the Marriott's business, Marriott International acquired the Ritz-Carlton Hotel Company, an up-market hotel chain known for beautiful locations and unparalleled service. We soon found ourselves doing some work for the brand. In preparation, I visited one of the chain's locations near its headquarters and was struck by how genuinely I was greeted and by the understated grace of the service. I made it a point to ask employees I met if they could describe the Ritz-Carlton Hotel Company culture. They all had the same genuine and endearing reply, "Oh, that's quite simple. *'We're ladies and gentlemen, serving ladies and gentlemen.'* I was struck by how clear the resolution was by the company's strong sense of identity and purpose. Looking further I discovered that this was part of a story told by the company's president, Horst Schulze.

I spoke to Mr. Schulze, a delightful and engaging man, who recounted his humble beginnings, being taken by his mother to a local hotel for an apprenticeship. While there he was made a busboy and sent to hotel school once a week. After some time, his instructor asked the class to write a story of their experiences at the hotel. Mr. Schulze wrote instinctively about the maître d' he worked for. He was an imposing and elegant man, meticulous and immaculate down to every detail. "He came to work to be excellent." Said Mr. Schulze, "He was a very proud man." He told Mr. Schulze that while people who stayed at the hotel were individuals of importance, namely *Ladies and Gentlemen*, service to them was not *servitude*. The maître d' insisted that Mr. Schulze could be very much a gentleman, as they were, by virtue of how excellent he was in the pursuit of his job. "I was told I could be a gentleman by creating excellence," Mr. Schulze recounted. He extolled the importance of humanity, which Mr. Schulze made a hallmark of his career, with wonderful thoughts like, "Elegance without warmth is arrogance."

Mr. Schulze captured this extraordinary sentiment in a simple yet penetrating thought, *Ladies and Gentlemen Serving Ladies and Gentlemen*. He could have said, "We are a company of elegance" or "Exacting Standards." He didn't. Instead he told a human story of an aspiring young man, prodded by the standards of excellence set by his mentor, redefining himself as a gentleman. Mr. Schulze was very astute, not just for his beliefs and business acumen but in his storytelling ability and careful use of language.

The HerdBuoys Story

In the discussion earlier about the real ambition, I recounted a story. It was a story about how an ambition was turned into a great victory for a fledgling agency. I have encapsulated it into this short narrative. Here is a summary, using all the tools of story.

In the days before freedom for black people in South Africa, three men set out to change their country. They formed an agency struggling with no accounts save a voter registration effort for their country that earned them no revenue. After years of struggle came their first few accounts and then management takeover and formation of Herdbuoys McCann. It was a short while later that the opportunity of a lifetime presented itself: a pitch for South African Airways. Earnest in their efforts to pitch, they were seriously behind until twenty-four hours before the day, when a small piece of film crystallized their dreams and ambitions, not just for themselves but for a new unified nation of South Africa. This little bit of footage and its accompanying lullaby changed the course of South Africa's future, its national airline reflecting the sentiments of a newly unified nation created by HerdBuoys, a little company but a living reflection of this ambition.

All of the elements are there: the core, credo, real ambition, conceptual target, and the hidden agenda, as well as a careful argument for the shaping of a new South Africa...but now... the elements are told as a compelling, endearing, inspiring story.

Happy Ntshingila, who you may recall was one of the founders of HerdBuoys, wrote some years later in his wonderful book, *Black Jerusalem*, of the agency's journey. Toward the end is a moving summary of this wonderful story:

I remember the holes in the soles of one of my decent pair of black shoes, the consequence of attending function after function in an attempt to drum up business in the early days. On one occasion my wife even refused to accompany me to one such function because she was embarrassed by "those shoes."

I thought of the successful pitch for South African Airways. I did not think of the problems ahead as chronicled earlier. I

*thought of the people behind the pitch both on the client side
and on the agency side.*

*It dawned on me that something bigger happened today,
bigger than just the winning of one piece of business.*

*One of the earliest definitions of Jerusalem is a "legacy
of peace." I like that definition ... Believe me brothers and sisters,
no two words have more simpatico in Africa than peace and hope."*

Okay, Here's How

First, identify the essential elements of your story:

1. What opposing forces or villains do you face?
2. What will you draw on? *(Clue: it is your* core)
3. What is your quest? *(Clue: it is your* real ambition)
4. Who are the heroes? *(Clue: they're you and your audience!)*
5. What values and beliefs sustain your journey? *(Clue: this
   is your* credo)
6. What is at stake? What is the desire? *(Clue: it is the* hidden agenda)
7. How will the story be resolved? What does the future
   portend?

Writing your pitch story involves taking the work that you
have done in building your argument—based on the lessons
we've learned from the *advocate's approach*—and crafting it into
a compelling story with all the above elements. As an example,
do you remember Company A in chapter 6? Earlier, we took
their stated mission, and wrote a compelling real ambition
statement:

To business adventurers, Company A will be a pioneer that creates technical leaps for people's most precious needs, because of a belief that scientific advancement is a gift in the service of humankind.

So let's construct Company A's story:

Each and every day a voice is heard, speaking for the fundamental gifts of life. Clean water. A healthy child. The opportunity to learn. The keys to these things can be found in the secrets of science. We are on a journey of discovery toward a means to unlock these mysteries. Wherever the road ahead may turn, for us, it leads to only one place, to the advancement of life one person at a time.

Okay, I'm in.

Let's deconstruct the elements:

Hero: Company A, an outwardly focused pioneer concerned about the world around it
The Villain: The world's blights
Quest: To unlock the mysteries of science
Reversal: The unknown roads ahead
Dénouement: The benefit of human beings, one person at a time

Let yourself go. Take the essential elements of your argument and let your heart do the talking.

Red Lion Square

I had my dream job. An office in London. Jetting between Europe, the Middle East, and Africa. Living in the city of BBC broadcasts. On this particular day I was on my way to lead a pitch in London for a major technology company. I jumped in the car to drive to the pitch. I looked at the address in the dossier: 26 Red Lion Sq. WC2. It couldn't be. I would be returning to virtually the same spot where I'd stood nearly twenty-five years before. As I made my way into the boardroom, my carefully prepared opening went right out the window.

I began, "Good morning. I have a confession to make. I had prepared quite an opener for you this morning, and it was all about ambition, the ambition you've outlined and our shared ambition as partners. But instead, my friends, I simply must share this with you." I pointed to the window looking out over Red Lion Square. "If you look out this window, you will see number seven Tresham House. It's a council flat, and twenty-five years ago as a young student I lived in that room right there. The Fryer's Delight around the corner on Theobald's Road was, and I know still is, the very best fish and chips in town. The interior is unchanged except for the labels over the prices (then, cod and chips was 50p). As I struggled with living away from home for the very first time in a new and unfamiliar place, at a time when I had little in my pocket, I dreamed of this moment. I have to say that, no matter what may be, win or lose, I hope you know that being here means more you could ever know, that I thank you for affording me and my team this moment."

My impromptu but heartfelt story of my own real ambition captivated the group. Cable and Wireless did award us the business, and we celebrated with a plate of cod, chips, and mushy peas.

REMEMBER THIS

Storytelling is the delivery of passion, emotion, and desire. Your pitch, to move to emotion from theorem and logic, must be woven into an audience-riveting story. Storytelling is persuasive because it involves the human condition: heroes, villains, plot complications, struggles, journeys, and redemption. Your pitch is not a recitation of fact; instead, your pitch must carry your audience with you by touching and moving them profoundly.

Conclusion

· · · · · · · · · · · · · · ·

I heard many things as a kid, not the least of which was the need to "practice what you preach." So, I bring our time together, and my story, to a close. Perhaps the most critical point in my career, October 22, 1997, was a day that changed a lot of lives. It could have been much, much different. MasterCard executive Larry Flanagan and his colleagues could have chosen the safe and certain path. Instead, they were brave and followed their instincts, embracing a simple gut feeling that our "Priceless" campaign reflected what was really in the hearts of their audience and believing that my colleagues and I were people who understood their hidden agenda.

Fifteen years later, the results of this fateful decision are staggering. The "Priceless" campaign appears regularly in upwards of 110 countries. Hundreds of TV commercials in dozens of languages have aired. A public offering of Master-Card was highly successful, and now MasterCard represents a formidable rival to Visa; it's come a long, long way from a brand and a company teetering on the brink. All this resulted, I believe, because of people's ability to understand what lies in another's heart and to connect to it. Over my span of years in the advertising business, I developed the ability to step back and see the patterns, and they are clear to me. When you can see, with x-ray clarity, the deep, visceral, emotional motivation that lies in the heart of your audience—the hidden agenda— you can move mountains. Businesses are won and followings created by simple acts of human empathy. When you can see past the surface and unlock the emotional desires of your prospects, the world is your oyster.

It seems crazy for an adman to assert that we don't really "persuade" anybody to do anything. I believe, however, that businesses hire you and people follow you not because they've had their arms twisted, but because they see that you understand them, that you have devoted the time and the sensitivity needed to empathize with their yearnings, and that you possess a special gift that can help them reach their hearts' desires.

If you connect your credo, your core, and your real ambition to your constituency, create an ironclad argument via the advocate's approach, and then tell a compelling story of an exciting future that achieves their hidden agenda, you can move mountains.

In our journey together we have examined several crucial principles of crafting a winning pitch. The search for the *hidden agenda* is the search for desire, and this agenda is rarely in evidence. You will need to put on special antennae to receive these signals. There is no trickery or hidden persuasion needed to find your audience's hidden agenda; what is required is emotional insight, human sensitivity, thoughtfulness, empathy, and *very* good listening skills. These can be applied in a scientific approach that may require a bit of "unlearning" of previous ways and means to pitch. This fundamental concept is even more potent when creating a following among a large and disparate group. The *conceptual target* offers a means to create a powerfully motivating, hidden agenda–inspired definition of your constituency.

Your *core*, *credo*, and *real ambition* are what I call *leverageable assets*. They are the means by which you bond with your audience. This key step is the moment of truth, more important than any other step in the process, because the insights that you have gleaned into the hidden agenda of your audience is the foundation upon which your approach is based.

To be understood, for people to grasp what you are saying and follow your argument, you must be as clear as you are compelling. The magic in *the advocate's approach* lies in compelling clarity that comes from crystal clear logic. This is a critical reduction to an essential core that can be shared and understood by virtually all constituencies.

In this new world, the message is not *buy* me, it's *join* me. You cannot demand your audience's attention. But you can ignite it, through the time-honored practice of *storytelling*, which reaches to the heart of your audience's desire and connects profoundly to it. When you do this, people will follow you. They will embrace you and anything you represent, whether it is the direction of your company, the project you lead, or the product you sell

I suppose there is no better and more appropriate way for me to finalize my case than to take a cue from the memorable campaign of which I was proud to be a part:

Pitches undertaken: scores
Fine companies encountered: hundreds
Amazing people met: thousands
Helping people achieve what matters most to them
    through their hidden agendas: priceless

Epilogue

. . . .

I hope you've enjoyed the journey as much as I have and, most importantly, have a fresh new tool for winning. You will win business and create a following by touching the heart of your audience's hidden agenda and connecting to it profoundly. The process isn't just a formal, once-in-a-blue-moon affair. It includes the informal meetings that we have with colleagues and clients each and every day, as well as the momentous acts, where we must lead huge organizations to accomplish the seemingly impossible. It is all a matter of stirring people to join you and to act. When you uncover the unspoken desire your audience holds dear and promise a journey that imagines the realization of this desire, they will travel with you.

I began our time together with my ideas about what I thought this book might represent, a sort of mentorship. I suppose there is no better way to conclude our time together than to quote those who have helped and influenced me along my journey. I wish you every possible success, and sincerely hope that the concepts and the tools I've shared will help you. And so, what better way to close than with a few words from my mentors...

Epilogue

"It's very simple, Kevin, it's about wants and desires. A young mother may want a set of encyclopedias, but she desires for her kid to become president."

—Enid Merin

"Growing a business is all about shoe leather."

—Harry Delaney

"Step out from behind that suit and be yourself. It is what we all want to see and love about you."

—Bill Genge

"Oh, geez, I'm a bundle of noives."

—Aunt Franny

"Only when you do a bit of digging can you reveal what is really going down. You've got to be one part cop, two parts priest, and five parts shrink."

—Uncle Don

"Kevin, if you believe in something enough, you can make it happen, but in doing so you will get knocked down...and often. This isn't the test of your strengths. The test is the fact that you keep getting up again."

—Grandpa Whalen

"Don't worry about how other people are doing things. Just do things in your own special way."

—Peter Kim

"Be good. Don't hit and play nice with the other children."

—Joan Allen

Best wishes to you all.

Further Reading

My Favorites

Angelou, Maya, *2009. Letter to My Daughter.* New York: House.

Cook, Roy J. 1958. *One Hundred and One Famous Poems.* Chicago: Contemporary Books.

Fulghum, Robert. 1989. *All I Really Need to Know I Learned in Kindergarten.* New York: Villard Books.

Saint-Exupéry, Antoine de. 1945. *The Little Prince.* London: Mammoth Press.

Leadership

Brent, Mike, and Fiona Elsa Dent. 2010. *The Leader's Guide to Influence.* Harlow, UK: Prentice Hall.

Giuliani, Rudolph W. 2002. *Leadership.* New York: Hyperion.

Marriott, J.W., and Kathi Ann Brown. 1997. *The Spirit to Serve: Marriott's Way.* New York: HarperCollins.

Further Reading

The Pitch

Bayley, Stephen, and Roger Mavity. 2007. *Life's a Pitch*. London: Corgi Books.

Guber, Peter. 2011. *Tell to Win*. New York: Crown Business.

Steel, Jon. 2007. *Perfect Pitch*. Hoboken, NJ: Wiley.

Selling

Blount, Jeb. 2010. *People Buy You*. Hoboken, NJ: Wiley.

Gitomer, Jeffrey. 2005. *Little Red Book of Selling*. Austin, TX: Bard Press.

Storytelling

Truby, John. 2007. *The Anatomy of Story*. New York: Faber and Faber.

Litigation

Scalia, Antonin, and Bryan A. Garner. 2008. *Making Your Case: The Art of Persuading Judges*. St. Paul, MN: Thompson.

Personal Branding

Kaputa, Catherine. 2010. *U R a Brand*. Boston: Nicholas Brealey.

Decision Making

Gigerenzer, Gerd. 2008. *Gut Feelings*. London: Penguin.

Social Marketing

Weber, Larry 2011, *Everywhere: Comprehensive Digital Business Strategy for the Social Media Era*. New York: John Wiley & Sons.

Further Reading

Negotiating

Fisher, Roger, William Ury, and Bruce Patton. 1991. *Getting to Yes*. New York: Penguin.

Special People

Ntshingila, Happy. 2009. *Black Jerusalem*. Capetown: Umuzi.

Index

Index

Charbit, Gerard, 36–37
"Chief medical officer" conceptual
    target, 50
China Mobile, 195–196
Churchill, Winston, 43
Citizenships, 49
Clinton, Bill, 47–48
Coca-Cola, 20, 165
Communication, 70
Company
    contact strategy for learning
        about, 74–75
    internal materials from, 74
    publishings from, 72
Conceptual target/targeting
    "chief medical officer," 50
    definition of, 40–41, 57
    description of, 206–207
    descriptors of, 49–50
    for Ericsson, 55–57
    evolution of, 44–45
    examples of, 51–57
    following, 43–44
    for Marriott International,
        51–52
    for MasterCard, 52–55
    origins of, 45–47
    principles associated with,
        40–41
    "self-made visionary," 50
    "soccer moms," 41,
        47–48
    writing of, 50–51
Confide, 173–178
Contact strategy, 74–75
Context, 27
Core
    connecting the, 83–84
    definition of, 104

finding your. *See* Finding your
    core
identifying with, 86
needs and, connection between,
    155
in win strategy for MasterCard,
    161
Corporate culture, 88
Cranin, Jonathan, 54
CreditSuisse, 5
Credo
    associative method for
        identifying, 118–120
    connection to values, 155
    definition of, 103, 105, 112–113
    family, 118, 121–122
    of Johnson & Johnson, 114–115,
        175, 177
    of Marriott International, 111,
        156, 162
    projective methods for
        identifying, 120–121
    writing of, 121

D
Dawes, Cris, 196–197
Delaney, Harry, 85–86, 210
Democratization, 49
Demographics, 44
Dénouement, 191
Desire, 23–25, 59, 206
Deutsche Bank, 5
DISC, 99
Discovery, 172
DiSesa, Nina, 179
Distillation, 151
Drama, 194–195
Dreams, 127

216

Index

Index

Index

values as, 28–29
wants as, 28
Myers-Briggs Type Indicator, 99

N
Nair, Suresh, 53, 179
Needs
  core connected to, 155
  description of, 28
  questions for triggering
    responses about, 69
  statements focusing on, 35
Nestlé, 5
New York City, 32–33, 113, 128,
  142
Noble intentions, 136
Nokia, 151
Ntshingila, Happy, 129–131, 200

O
Okon, Joe, 98
Opel, 5
Opening statement, 172
Oral argument, 168

P
Pepsi, 20
Perfect Man, 86–90, 103
Pernod Ricard, 151
Personal appearance, 86–87
Personality profile, 66
Pfizer, 5
Picture sort, for finding your core, 95
Pitch/pitching
  as argument, 166
  facts and evidence used in, 172

importance of, 7–8
in intimate setting, 39
to Irish Tourist Board, 185–187
to Johnson & Johnson, 116–117,
  173–178
logic path used in, 172
to MasterCard, 2, 5, 20–23,
  36–37, 54–55, 93–94, 173,
  181–182, 205
opening statement of, 172
to South African Airways,
  132–133, 200
summation of, 172–173
traditional presentation of, 171
to Unilever, 134–135
Please Understand Me, 99
Plummer, Joe, 45, 48
Positivity, 24
"Priceless" campaign, 2, 5, 20–23,
  36–37, 54–55, 93–94, 181–182,
  205
Profile/profiling
  creating of, 100
  example of, 101–102
  finding your core through,
    98–100
Projective methods
  for finding your core, 93–96
  for identifying your credo,
    120–121
Prospect
  asking questions, 67–70
  body language by, 64
  emotional closeness with, 62
  emotions of, 64–65, 67
  initial meeting with, 62–63
  interrogation of, 63
  listening to, 63–64, 66–67
  personality profile of, 66

Index

Index

Index

Introduce Kevin and his powerful approach to your organization

Kevin's keynote speaker events and programs leave participants inspired to believe that they can accomplish anything and equipped to do the job brilliantly.

Kevin Allen Keynotes:

THE HIDDEN AGENDA:
A Proven Way to Win business and Create a Following
Pitches are made in business every day—to win the account, convince a colleague or sell a vision to the Board of Directors, but people ignore the most basic component of making the sale—decisions are made by people. Kevin Allen has recognized that by identifying the needs -spoken or unspoken- of your audience and connecting the pitch directly to it, you win. In this compelling presentation, you'll learn in concrete terms how- not to persuade-but to compel people to follow you.

CREATING WINNERS:
The Market Imperative:
Kevin shows business leaders how to infuse the spear point of what the company brings to the market as the ultimate galvanizer. He brings unity of purpose by looking through the lens of the marketplace at the only audience that matters— the ultimate customer. Participants leave highly motivated by the knowledge that who they are and what they believe connects with their company's customer and how this will lead their company to win.

Find out more about bringing Kevin to your organization.
Contact Kevin at Nicola@kevinallenpartners.com

About the Author's Work with Clients

Kevin Allen is the CEO and Founder of KevinAllen-Partners, a unique company dedicated to transforming the way companies grow.

With global go-to-market consulting, executive and team coaching, business development training and large-scale change and performance enhancement programs, KevinAllenPartners show talented people and teams how they can ignite a company's greatness.

K → **Keynote**
& Employee Motivation

A → **Ambition**
& Go-To-Market Planning

P → **Professional Development**
& Training

Learn how KevinAllenPartners can help your company achieve more than you previously thought possible by contacting Kevin and his team directly at www.kevinallenpartners.com

Additional Resources from Kevin Allen

*Visit www.KevinAllenPartners.com to view
supporting videos from Kevin that expand on
some of the key concepts throughout the book.*

Pure Growth

How To Pitch and Win

Real Ambition

Credo

Core

The Advocates Approach

Storytelling

Made in the USA
Middletown, DE
09 July 2019